DISCARDED

JOLLY ROGER with an UZI

JOLLY ROGER
WITH AN UZI

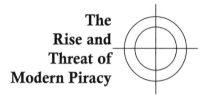

The Rise and Threat of Modern Piracy

Jack A. Gottschalk and Brian P. Flanagan
with Lawrence J. Kahn and Dennis M. LaRochelle

Naval Institute Press *Annapolis, Maryland*

Naval Institute Press
291 Wood Road
Annapolis, MD 21402

Library of Congress Cataloging-in-Publication Data
Gottschalk, Jack A.

    Jolly Roger with an Uzi : the rise and threat of modern piracy / Jack
    A. Gottschalk and Brian P. Flanagan with Lawrence J. Kahn and Dennis
    M. LaRochelle.

    p.   cm.
    Includes bibliographical references (p.   ) and index.
    ISBN 1-55750-328-1 (acid-free paper)
    1. Pirates. 2. Hijacking of ships. 3. Terrorism. I. Flanagan, Brian P.,
    1955– . II. Title.
    HV6441.G67 2000
    364.16'4—dc21   99-40339

To Mom, who has always been there, and to Claudia, who was there at the beginning of this project in August 1996 at the South Street Seaport

—*Jack A. Gottschalk*

To my father, Jerome V. Flanagan, who never dictated to me where I had to learn or what I had to learn, but was always there to help me learn, and to my wife, Corinne, for her patience, understanding, and support when I get involved in one of these projects

—*Brian P. Flanagan*

Contents

Foreword

There is a common perception in many quarters that the problem of piracy is a thing of the past. In this case, perception is far removed from reality.

Not only is high-seas piracy a continuing problem, but criminal acts against vessels within coastal state territorial seas and internal waters are also occurring with increasing frequency. Since 1995, the International Maritime Organization (IMO) has issued monthly and quarterly reports of piracy and armed robbery incidents, many of which have taken place while vessels were in port.

Overall, the number of incidents has been increasing, and nations have found that cooperation between coastal and port nations is necessary to address the piracy problem wherever it is found. In November 1998, the sixty-ninth United Nations General Assembly, in its Oceans and Law of the Sea Resolution, called on all countries to take necessary action to prevent and combat piracy and armed robbery at sea. In addition, the UN called upon countries to cooperate fully with the IMO in these matters.

In order for there to be an effective response to this growing problem, there will need to be a considerable degree of cooperation among coastal states, port states, and flag states—those countries where a vessel is registered.

Since obtaining the kind of cooperation adequate to effectively address this growing problem will be both slow and difficult, education of the public may be the most effective step that can be taken in the short term.

The purpose of this book is to provide an historical perspective on piracy, to examine its modern dimensions, and to consider what can be done about the problem. While the book is not intended to provide a detailed analysis of international law, the authors review applicable maritime statutes. By examining the operations of modern-day pirates and the efforts of governments and industry to address the problem, the authors provide a valuable resource for those who are concerned with developing policy regarding maritime crime.

Michael Boock
Adjunct professor,
George Washington University School of Law

Introduction

Pirates! The age-old warning cry still has the power to evoke feelings of danger and excitement. From time immemorial, writers have introduced us to real and fictional pirates of every kind and have described the hoards of treasures they accumulated. For many people, the demise of the imaginary Captain Hook in *Peter Pan* marked their last thoughts of pirates and piracy.

But piracy is real and it is a serious, and most often violent, crime made particularly onerous because it occurs in a maritime environment that is dangerous in itself.

Pirates and piracy, despite the violence that has been associated throughout history with both the perpetrators and the activity, have achieved a romantic aura much like the highwaymen who plagued eighteenth-century England and the bank, train, and stagecoach bandits who prowled the American West.

History has given us a long list of pirates that includes such questionable luminaries as Henry Morgan, Jean Laffite, Edward Teach (also known more popularly as Blackbeard),

Captain Kidd and—not to be accused or found guilty of male chauvinism—Anne Bonny. These and other pirates still hold the public imagination as being, despite their villainous and generally felonious actions, brave and highly independent characters who somehow managed to prevail (at least for a limited time) against heavy odds.

The grim fact, of course, is that despite the romantic allure, pirates are simply an oceangoing breed of robbers and killers. From the days of the Phoenicians and Vikings to the present, violence and blood have been the trademarks and the common bond of piracy.

Today, pirates are back and with a vengeance, motivated by the same desperate greed as their predecessors of yesteryear and attacking their victims with no less violence. Piracy occurs worldwide. The targets of the modern-day buccaneers range from supertankers to small pleasure craft. Murder and serious bodily injury are common elements of this maritime criminal behavior.

Today's pirates by broad definition include drug smugglers, organized-crime groups, individual "entrepreneurs," and terrorists, all of whom have found this kind of activity to be a good fit to their talents and liking. In some parts of the world, the new pirates have gained access to specialized (and, presumably confidential) information about cargoes, and they have connections to the government agencies that control and monitor the movement of ships through some of the busiest ports on the globe.

In this book we are not set on a course that will add to any romantic assessment of pirates. We begin with a very general overview of piracy from ancient days in the Mediterranean, on the waters of northern Europe and Southeast Asia, and move through the Tudor years of Drake and Hawkins into what is commonly termed the "Golden Age" of piracy. This brief historical glimpse at piracy and pirates then continues into the nineteenth century and recent times.

We look at the relevant law of the sea and the law as it applies to pirates. In order to provide what we sincerely hope is a complete view of the problem today, we examine the issue of piracy in terms of both its human and economic costs. As part of our examination, we have looked at the links between piracy and international politics and at other possible connections, particularly those between land-based and seagoing criminals and criminal groups. And, in the world as it exists today, we have deemed it necessary to examine the problem of maritime terrorism. Our belief is that while terrorism is not part of the classical definition of piracy, it cannot be ignored when seriously discussing deliberately created dangers on the waterways of the globe. Finally, we have not forgotten the potential perils that can be and are posed by piracy not only to individual victims and to property but also to the environment, and thus all of us, as a whole.

One highly possible, and chilling, example will most surely suffice. A single ship, loaded with some lethal cargo, is seized, its crew disabled or removed, and left adrift as a menace to navigation and to the environment. One need not possess an overactive imagination to envision a loaded supertanker or, as another and even more vivid example, a carrier of liquid natural gas (LNG) as the unlucky vessel described here.

Our thesis is simple. The problem of piracy is a major one that, despite articles in many general-circulation publications, is being largely ignored. People are being killed by pirates and ships are being seized. The fact that modern pirates (or terrorists) no longer fit the description of Captain Kidd, complete with cutlass and flintlock, does not change their fundamental criminal intent.

We will seek to provide some suggestions for solution of the problem, although we recognize that solutions are far more easy to propose than to adopt, particularly when dealing with a problem that requires international cooperation. At the very least we seek to illuminate a major issue and to generate more public and governmental interest. If that goal is attained, the result could be a reduction in the level of piracy activity worldwide and thus in the danger posed to seafarers, property, the environment, and, of course, to all of us.

Before entering the world of modern piracy and maritime terrorism, it is necessary to name some of the people who have contributed to this project. In alphabetical order, our most sincere thanks go to Charles Barthold, John Grissom, Pierce Hoover, Joseph Mignon, Lou Mizell, Terry Parham, Pierre Pierce, Bill Pike, Lt. Richard Pineiro, USCG, David Truitt, and Capt. Bruce Weule, USCG (Ret.). All of these individuals were gracious enough to donate their valuable time to provide guidance and to link our questions with answers. Additional thanks go to Eric Ellen of the International Maritime Bureau; to Matthew Marshall of the Institute of London Underwriters; and to the law firm of Orrick, Herrington & Sutcliffe, LLP. And, thanks also to Gerald J. DeBenedette and John West for their computer-based research and to the staffs of both the Drew University library, and the Livingston, NJ, Public Library—the latter being where research for this book began.

Finally, we owe very special thanks to Dennis M. La-Rochelle for the excellent chapter on the economic impact of piracy, and to Lawrence J. Kahn for his input on the high cost of piracy in terms of both physical and psychological trauma suffered by its human victims.

If anyone was left off the list who should have been there, the absence was unintentional and the thanks are no less sincere.

JOLLY ROGER with an UZI

The Evolution of Piracy

I t is generally accepted that piracy became a major problem as soon as, and wherever, maritime commerce existed.[1] In more common parlance that translates to mean that the very first time something valuable was known to be leaving a beach on a raft the first pirate was around to steal it. While history contains no information about such initial waterborne felonies, records of piracy have been found among the Phoenicians and the Greeks.[2]

As the pirate menace grew, efforts were made to suppress it. Attempts were made by Crete and Athens, and by the Rhodians, who were the first to codify the law of the sea.[3] The success of these antipiracy campaigns was neither significant nor permanent. Until Rome became the unquestioned power of the Mediterranean, pirates plundered at will, taking full advantage of the Punic Wars. It is claimed that one of the earliest and best known of pirate victims was a young Julius Caesar who was held for ransom in about 75 B.C. Allegedly, Caesar later captured the pirates and had them crucified.[4] The story, of course, may not be completely factual—a point that should be kept in mind when dealing with much pirate and related literature and history.

As Rome's naval power grew, its leaders embarked on a serious program designed to eliminate piracy from the Mediterranean. In 67 B.C., Pompey the Great created a maritime patrol force that was successful in reducing the threat of piracy to Roman commerce. The pirates, however, were a truly organized force and more than patrols were needed to provide a permanent and long-range solution.[5]

It was not until 10 A.D., under Emperor Augustus, that Rome's full naval power was arrayed against the pirates. Effective control, once established, was maintained for almost three hundred years.

PIRATES IN NORTHERN WATERS

The Mediterranean was not the only area of the early world that witnessed pirate activity. For two centuries the Vikings and oceanborne thieves from the British Isles were at work not only on the North Sea and in the Baltic, but on the Elbe and Rhine Rivers, as well. Commerce was so negatively affected that the principal reason for the creation of the Hanseatic League in the twelfth century was the suppression of piracy.

ASIA AND THE MIDDLE EAST

Chinese, Japanese, and Malayan pirates operated throughout the Indian Ocean, the South China Sea, and adjacent waters at least as early as the fourteenth century. By the end of the fifteenth century, piracy had achieved such prominence that it was the target of the Ming Dynasty, which mounted a force against it that included 3,100 warships, 400 armed transports, and more than 30,000 men.[6]

Japanese pirates, much like their Western counterparts, operated as both legitimate traders and, when times were hard, as pirates. In another similarity, the Japanese pirates were sometimes financed by various warlords and merchants.

From earliest times, the waters off Africa and of the Persian Gulf were infested with pirates. They raided coastal settlements, took captives to be ransomed or sold as slaves, and caused havoc on the high seas.

THE MEDITERRANEAN MIDDLE AGES

Sailing from ports along the North African coast, Muslim pirates (known as corsairs by the French) raided the shores of southern Europe and ravaged maritime commerce during the Middle Ages. They, too, seized captives (mostly Christians) and either held those victims for ransom or sold them to the Turks.

During the fourteenth century when the Ottoman Turks were seeking to control the Mediterranean, the North African pirates were allied with them. The glory days for these pirates ended with the Christian defeat of the Turks at the Battle of Lepanto in 1571. Despite this setback, however, the pirates remained a threat until defeated by the Americans at Tripoli in 1805 and, more significantly, by the French conquest of much of North Africa in 1830.

PRIVATEERS AND BUCCANEERS

Historians have written more about the pirates who first gained prominence in sixteenth-century England than about earlier ones. The simple reason is that far more is known about them. The names and deeds of pirates such as Henry Morgan, Edward Teach (Blackbeard), and Captain William Kidd are first encountered by most of us in grade school, if not through books, television, and movies. They are the stuff of romantic drama.

Most, but not all, of those who became pirates in the late-sixteenth and early-seventeenth centuries began their activities as privateers commissioned (mostly by the English) to seek out, seize, and destroy all things having to do with the Spanish enemy.[7] This was a particularly appealing opportunity for those selected to operate under such color of authority. Spanish ships were plentiful and were transporting huge quantities of gold and silver to the New World.

Most of the privateers sailed from ports in England or along the Atlantic coast in their search for Spanish (and, later, Dutch and French) ships. Many privateering veterans (almost all of them Protestant) somehow settled on the island of Hispaniola in the Caribbean during the mid-seventeenth century. Their principal activity was the hunting and roasting of wild animals. The Spanish considered them as both heretics and illegal inhabitants of lands claimed by Spain as part of its Roman Catholic empire.

Mutual hatred was established early and the "buccaneers," as they would be called, from the words used by the French to describe "roasters of meat," soon turned their hunting talents from animals to Spanish ships.[8]

The Spanish remained the principal targets of these "Brethren of the Coast" (another name for the Caribbean-based pirates) until the end of conflict between England and Spain in 1692. When peace was declared, those wanting to remain in the vocation needed to increase their activities and when that occurred, the Golden Age of piracy (1692–1725) began.[9]

Pirate activity began to expand almost immediately after the conflict between England and Spain ended and included attacks on shipping of all nations to include the huge treasure-carrying transports that sailed the waters of the Indian Ocean and the Red Sea. This territorial expansion from what had previously been principally limited to the Atlantic and the Caribbean required a new base to rest and take on needed supplies. The pirates found this on Madagascar and, over time, it became their domain. But it was harder to be a pirate in the absence of those Spanish treasure ships and without the possibility of holding a privateer's commission that provided an official blessing for robbery and murder on the high seas.

Fortunately for the pirates, the War of the Spanish Succession, which pitted the English and the Dutch against Spain and France, reopened opportunities for both privateering and piracy.[10] The war, which began in 1701, lasted until 1713. When it ended, pirates and privateers were forced from Madagascar back to the Bahamas in the Caribbean. It was on the main Bahamian island of New Providence that the Golden Age would end, as will be later described.

PIRATICAL REQUIREMENTS

As with anyone who makes a living, criminals have certain fundamental requirements for success. Thus, pirates from the days of the Phoenicians and Vikings to now, wherever they are found, share some needs.

First, it makes no sense for pirates to prowl waterways where the pickings are not known to be very good. In short, if you are ready and willing to undertake the inherent risks of pirating, the rewards must be worthwhile.

Second, the geographic area where pirates prey must be one in which the risk level of detection is acceptable. It is not a good idea, for example, in modern times, to conduct piracy operations in a place such as the English Channel.

Third, if at all possible, there should be safe havens where a pirate can hide, seek repairs, and obtain supplies.

These considerations still apply. The need for both a relatively secluded area of operations and a secure place to hide is obvious to the pirates who are active in the Straits of Malacca and in the South China Sea.

THE TOOLS AND THE TALENT

The reasons why piracy became so widespread by the early 1700s are many and varied. First, as mentioned earlier, there were many wars involving the British, the French, the Spanish, and the Dutch. The conflicts were, to a large extent, naval ones and, not unlike most wars, their end caused many ships to be laid up and sailors to be laid off. Unemployed seamen often considered the risks of life as a pirate to be more than offset by the potential rewards.

It is also true, all other things being equal, that life aboard many a pirate ship was a good deal better than it was on a merchant or naval vessel. The master of a merchant or naval ship held near-dictatorial powers over his crew. The typical sailor received low pay, endured terrible living and working conditions, and could be lashed for minor infractions. While life on a pirate ship or privateer was also austere, most crew members shared the profits of the enterprise. Moreover, except during actual combat, pirate ships operated largely on democratic principles. Floggings were rarely employed and discipline tended to be lax.

Finally, technology was making piracy easier. Navigation, a science whose development is generally credited to Prince Henry of Portugal, was at least roughly understood by the late fifteenth century. While the modern sextant and chronometer did not arrive on the maritime scene until the eighteenth century, there were some instruments in use such as the cross-staff, sundial, and astrolabe, a primitive sextant.[11] Additionally, charts were more accurate, ship hull designs were improving, and better systems of rigging permitted the increased use of bigger, more efficient sails.[12]

Faster, more-seaworthy ships; better navigation; a moderately well-trained and profit-motivated labor pool; and many ships laden with treasure a thousand miles from their home ports—the ingredients for piracy on a worldwide scale were all present.

THE GOLDEN AGE OF PIRACY

There are, in truth, several other important points that tended to make the Golden Age of piracy different from what had come before it. For one thing, any would-be pirate had to face the initial problem of getting a ship. In ancient times, the vessels used for, in most cases, both trade and piracy, were constructed as group projects and they were relatively simple to build. In the case of the Mediterranean pirates, those who built the boats were essentially part of a government.

By the time of the Golden Age, any good, seagoing ship that was desired by a pirate to sail anywhere in the world, had to be relatively large (hopefully big enough to be considered, at least at a distance, as a harmless merchantman); fast (enough to catch a victim); easy to handle (so as to evade a warship); and able to carry numerous cannon, the purpose of that being obvious. Given this initial requirement, the barrier to entry (using a modern business school term) to the piracy business could be a difficult one to overcome.

In fact, there were only two realistic ways to get a pirate ship or at least a ship able to become such a vessel. The first was to have been a privateer or buy a license to become one, and then have the ship and all supplies provided and financed by the government.

Another way of obtaining a suitable vessel was simply to steal one, generally a fast and well-equipped merchant ship. It was possible to take such a ship from a dock by overpowering the crew or to have enough people on board when it sailed to commit mutiny and take command on the high seas.

The second problem was obtaining guns, powder, and cannon balls. This hurdle had to be overcome immediately. Merely raising a pirate flag was certainly not going to be enough to cause a merchant ship to surrender. There had to be some muscle to go with the threat.

A solution to the problem was again found in one of two ways. If the would-be pirate were a privateer, he would have been supplied with the guns and ammunition by the government. If the pirate stole a ship he had to be certain that it was already armed.

Seizing a merchant ship that came complete with guns was, in reality, no harder to do than taking one that did not. Most merchant ships were armed because they were concerned about pirates. In fact, until well into the nineteenth century, ships that plied the waters of Southeast Asia had their hulls painted with false gun ports so as to look like warships, specifically, frigates.

As a final thought on the guns, there is some belief that the gunnery skills of many pirate crews were at least equal to those of some of the naval ships of the time. Most pirates did not want to test their skills in such a one-on-one contest. They felt, with justification, that a navy could afford to lose a battle while the pirates had to win every time.

THE PIRATE FLAG

It would be incomplete (if not unforgivable) to write about pirates and not include the famous (and equally infamous) pirate flag, known generally as the Jolly Roger.

While the well-known skull and crossbones emblem was, in fact, used by pirates, there were many variants of it with virtually all of them having a specific reference to death, such as a skeleton. When a pirate ship was ready to make its attack on a victim, whatever national flag was being carried was hauled down and replaced by the dreaded symbol of doom.[13]

Its use was based on the assumption that upon sight of the flag resistance would cease and, in return, the attacking pirates would carry out no violence. Since there was no financial profit realized in killing or being killed, the practice of most pirates was to spare the lives of the crew and passengers of ships that complied with their demands without resistance. Of course, there were no guarantees; surrender could also be an invitation to death. By contrast, if the pirates hoisted a plain red flag (often after the victim began to fight), there was no promise of anything except that no quarter would be given.

PIRATE DISCIPLINE

Pirate crews generally represented the lower levels of society. Virtually all had experience as mariners. The maintenance of discipline among such a group would have been difficult in any environment but, on a ship, it was only possible through agreement. The captain had to have the crew on his side either through camaraderie or through fear. The only thing that would keep a pirate crew happy and motivated was, of course, realizing the financial rewards they had set out to obtain.

The democratic tone of pirate life was set early in every voyage with the writing out of the ship's articles. These were signed by all who served aboard the vessel. While each one of these documents was worded differently, the provisions were basically the same as follows:

1. Every man shall obey Civil Command. The captain shall have one full share and a half of all Prizes. (Usually this was actually a double share.)

2. If any man shall offer to run away, or keep any secret from the Company, he shall be maroon'd with one Bottle of Powder, one Bottle of Water, one small Arm and shot.

3. If any man shall steal any Thing in the Company, or gain, to the value of a Piece of Eight, he shall be marooned or shot.

4. That Man who shall strike another whilst these Articles are in force shall receive Moses Law (that is 40 stripes lacking 1 on the bare Back).

5. That Man that shall snap his Arms or smoak Tobacco in the Hold without a Cap to his pipe, or carry a Candle lighted without a Lanthorn, shall suffer the same Punishment as in the former article.

6. That Man that shall not keep his Arms clean, fit for an Engagement, or neglect his Business, shall be cut off from his Share and suffer such other Punishment as the Captain and the Company shall think fit.

7. If any Man shall lose a Joint in time of an Engagement he shall have 400 Pieces of Eight: if a limb, 800.

8. If at any time you meet with a prudent Woman that Man that offers to meddle with her without her consent shall suffer present death.[14]

With such rules the pirates went out to search for ships and treasure.

TARGETS OF PIRACY

The pirates of the Golden Age, like all of the pirates before them, pursued a variety of opportunities. Ships were, of course, the softest of all targets, and for the most obvious of reasons, those that carried gold and silver were the most desired prey of all.

Precious metals including coins were the best kind of treasure but jewels, rum, molasses, spices, and fine silks were among other valuable cargoes. Property other than coins had to be disposed of through land-based fences. There were many merchants, including some prominent American and British ones, who offered their services. The need for such "brokerage" has been a problem faced by thieves ever since anyone started to keep records about crime and criminals.

Other pirate targets were seacoast towns anywhere in the world—the less fortified and the more rich, the better. In the later years of the Golden Age, however, coastal fortifications began to seriously outgun any single naval vessel. These included most ships manned by pirates. Still, if a raid could provide sufficient real treasures of any kind, the risk might be taken.

THE MERCHANT FENCES

Many of the most illustrious families in colonial America were engaged as fences of pirate booty or openly supported pirate activity.[15] The names included such prominent ones as Phillips and Livingston of New York, along with others in Philadelphia, Boston, Newport, and Charleston, where piracy was aided and abetted in clear violation of the law.[16]

These people functioned as both legitimate merchants and illegitimate brokers of stolen property and were necessary to the success of pirates and piracy. They placed a value on the goods that included their fee and, after paying the pirates, they would resell the property at a profit.

THE PERILS OF PIRACY

In addition to the general rigors of life at sea in those days, there was the very real danger of losing one's life in a heavy storm. But without doubt, the greatest fear of pirates was not of weather but rather of being engaged by a warship. In most cases, the principal pirate nemesis was a naval frigate.

Frigates were not large ships but they were fast. Mounting between forty and fifty guns, they were built to legally raid commerce, to carry messages between ships of the line and between battle fleets and shore commanders, and to destroy pirates.

When considering that most pirate ships carried fewer guns and were not built for combat, the outcome of a confrontation between a frigate and a pirate ship was almost always sure, although not certain. The pirate Blackbeard, for example, managed to fight off the thirty-gun frigate, HMS *Scarborough* during one famous encounter off the Carolinas during May 1717. It should be noted, however, that Blackbeard's ship, *Queen Anne's Revenge,* mounted forty guns.[17]

A PIRATE'S WHO'S WHO

It can be safely assumed that there were hundreds of pirates who tried to make a living on the ocean during the Golden Age. Some of the most well known or, at least, most interesting pirates who roamed the seas during that period included John Avery, also known as Henry Every; Stede Bonnet; Anne Bonny; Mary Read; and John "Calico Jack" Rackam. (Bonny, Read, and Rackam, as will be seen, must be reviewed together.) Others were William Kidd, Edward Teach (Blackbeard), Thomas Tew, and Henry Morgan. There are, of course, others who could be legitimately added to this admittedly judgmental list.

John Avery, sometimes known as Henry Every, was born in Plymouth, England, between 1653 and 1665. He went to sea at an early age as a member of the Royal Navy, became an accomplished navigator, and subsequently served on several merchant ships including those operating in the slave trade.

It was as a result of these credentials that he obtained the position of first officer aboard the privateer, *Charles II.* Needing a ship of his own for piracy, Avery led a successful mutiny aboard the ship and renamed it the *Fancy.*

Avery then embarked on a career of piracy that might have resulted in riches. Eventually, through a proper application of funds in the right places, he might even have won a pardon for the bloodless mutiny. Among his first pirate victims, however, were several English ships, a fact that made Avery into a flat-out criminal in the eyes of King William's government in England.

In August 1695, two treasure ships, the *Fateh Mohamed* and the *Gang-I-Sawai,* both flying the flag of the Great Mogul (the Muslim ruler of India), were sighted in the Red Sea. Avery attacked the boats and, in addition to taking gold, silver, and other cargo valued then at approximately 325,000 pounds sterling, he tortured and murdered many of the crew who had surrendered after his display of the red (no quarter) flag. The women found on board the seized ships were considered as a fringe benefit and were subjected in several cases to multiple rape.[18] One of those women was reported to be a relative of the Great Mogul.

This incident marked the "high" point of Avery's pirate career. Despite the mutiny, Avery rapidly became a popular hero, largely because of his courage and the damage he caused to the heathen Muslims. He became the real life model of a play and was the inspiration for a novel, *The Life, Adventures, and Pyracies of the Famous Captain Singleton,* written by Daniel DeFoe and published in 1720.

However, there was still the nagging problem of having pirated an English ship. For this no pardon was offered and Avery remained a wanted man in his home country.

It is believed that Avery did, finally, return to England and after that disappeared into history. There are those who claim that he died a poor man, and there are an equal number who say that Avery ended his days surrounded by the kind of splendor that he could, presumably, well afford.

Stede Bonnet had been a major in the British army and was the owner of a large plantation in Barbados. He was, however, unhappy with his lot in life and, specifically, with his wife. Bonnet began his career in 1716 by purchasing a pirate ship, a rather unusual beginning, and then openly recruiting a crew. He placed ten cannon on a ship that was designed for a single gun and went to sea.[19] Given just these facts it seems that Bonnet was lucky to get out of Bridgeton Harbor. Perhaps, in the end, drowning there would have been preferred to his hanging in Charleston in 1718.

Anne Bonny was born in Ireland. She was the illegitimate child of an attorney and the household maid. Anne, her father, and (presumably) the maid arrived in Charleston, South Carolina, about 1712. There she married a sailor and went with him to New Providence in the Bahamas sometime in 1716. At some point after that fateful arrival, she became the mistress and pirate associate of John "Calico Jack" Rackam, a linkage that would come to include Mary Read.

Rackam was in New Providence to obtain a pardon and a commission as a privateer. Instead, he and Anne stole a ship and went to sea as one of the most unusual pirate partnerships in history. One of their victims was a small Dutch merchant ship aboard which were several crew members who joined Rackam's vessel. Anne became attracted to a young member of the crew. Later, much to her presumed dismay, Anne discovered (the details on how are sketchy but can be imagined) that the target of her desire was actually another female pirate, Mary Read.

Mary, who was born somewhere in England around 1693, claimed that she was illegitimate and, for obscure reasons had been raised as a boy and subsequently served in the English army and in the Dutch merchant marine. Whatever the facts of her bizarre life, Mary Read sailed into history with Anne Bonny and John Rackam.

In 1720, after their capture near Jamaica, John Rackam was convicted of piracy and hanged. Anne Bonny, using her connections and those of her father with the South Carolina establishment, was released and returned to Charleston. Mary Read died in prison of a fever while awaiting execution.

Captain William Kidd makes the list because it is probably true that his name (and that of Blackbeard) would be most quickly identified with piracy by most people. And that is a curious fact because even though Kidd was hanged as a pirate, he may not really have been one.

In 1695, the East India Company, chartered by the English government and operating merchant ships throughout the Indian and Pacific oceans, was growing increasingly unhappy over the pirate menace. The company's ships were proving to be in constant danger and cargoes were being seized. It was, in short, a condition that was not good for business. King William, then engaged in yet another English-French war, did not want to reduce his naval forces by sending warships into what might well prove to be a long, costly, and frustrating campaign against pirates. In a moment of royal creativity, William conjured up a scheme that featured the licensing of a privateer whose job it would be to seek out and destroy pirates, many of whom were now using Madagascar as their base of operations.

At the instigation of the king, Thomas Livingston, a wealthy New Yorker, and Richard Coote, the Earl of Bellomont (and newly appointed colonial governor of New York), put together the necessary financing for such an antipirate project. They offered the post to Captain Kidd. A rough, semiliterate man, Kidd lived in New York and knew Livingston. Kidd was a shipowner, merchant, and former privateer of some note. Scottish-born in 1645, Kidd had emigrated to the colonies and married a wealthy young woman in New York.

In 1695, Kidd was bored, was available, and wanted a commission in the Royal Navy. He viewed this position as a possible avenue to that desired goal.

In August of that year, Kidd went to London and, to everyone's happiness, cut a deal with Livingston and Bellomont.

Then, as a newly appointed privateer and provided with a ship, *Adventure Galley,* mounting thirty-four guns, Kidd set out to seek and destroy French ships and capture pirates.

But Kidd's mission was difficult and the voyage troubled. Probably through error, he attempted the seizure of a vessel that turned out to be under English command. As frustration mounted among the members of his crew, so did confrontations with Kidd. One of those led to his striking a crewman on the head with a bucket and causing his death. On top of this, Kidd encountered a pirate on Madagascar whom he had known years before. Even though their relationship was edgy, Kidd failed to arrest him.

Despite all of these factors, Kidd set sail for home. Only after dropping anchor at Arguilla for supplies did he learn of his undesirable status. Kidd promptly sailed for New York and what he assumed would be the protection of both Livingston and Bellomont, the latter having taken up residence there as royal governor.

Kidd's faith in both Bellomont and Livingston is yet another example of his poor judgment. Upon arrival in New York, he found that Livingston refused to see him at all. Bellomont met with him and had him arrested. It appears that during Kidd's mission and absence, politics in London had raised its head and Parliament was now seeking to investigate the whole antipiracy scheme. Kidd was left to twist in the wind and that, in the end, became a literal, as well as a figurative, statement.

After his arrest, Kidd was sent to London for trial. He was held in Newgate prison from April 1700 to March 1701 when he was finally called to testify before Parliament concerning what would undoubtedly, in the present day, be dubbed "Kidd-gate."

Instead of taking a deal in which he would admit piracy in exchange for a pardon based on his testimony about the affair,

Kidd was uncooperative. He was then tried and convicted of piracy as well as for the murder of the crew member.

The execution was even more traumatic for Kidd than for most on the gallows. On 23 May 1701, he stepped off the plank at the Wapping Execution Dock and the rope broke. The second attempt at hanging was successful. Kidd's body was then tarred for preservation, placed in an iron cage, and displayed at the head of the Thames as a grim warning to all who might be tempted to engage in piracy—at least against the king's ships or those that fell under his protection.[20]

Edward Teach, known in popular lore as Blackbeard, was a murderous, sadistic, and probably psychopathic pirate who began his career as a privateer during the War of the Spanish Succession. Teach somehow wound up in Nassau about 1715. His exploits during the next three years were legendary and included the blockade of Charleston, South Carolina; seacoast raids from Virginia south into the Caribbean; the taking of scores of ships; and corrupt dealings with officials who, for a share of pirate booty, often provided pardons. But what makes Blackbeard of even more interest is how he died.

In November 1718, Teach and his crew were finally caught off Cape Hatteras by a British Navy expedition led by Lt. Robert Maynard. In hand-to-hand combat with pistol and cutlass, Maynard killed Teach and, as a symbol of total victory, cut off the pirate's head and threw the body into the water. Teach's head was then placed on the bowsprit of Maynard's ship as a trophy.[21]

Capt. Thomas Tew was born and spent a good part of his life in Newport, Rhode Island. Another, and significant, part of his existence was spent as a privateer in the services of the English government. To this man may well go the honor of being the seafarer who opened the Golden Age of piracy.

The privateering activities of Tew and others in colonial America must be measured against the political climate of the times. The hated Navigation Acts, which went into effect in 1651, blocked all colonial trade with any nation other than England. As a result, many highly desired imports were denied to the colonial population.

The inevitable "black market" for such goods, no matter how obtained by the merchants to sell and the consumers to purchase, offered fine opportunities for privateers. Much of this merchandise came from Spanish ships in the Caribbean.

But, as noted, the end of the war between England and Spain in 1692 put privateering in a state of disarray. At least that is how it affected some. Captain Tew was not one of them.

Tew was hired as a rather special kind of privateer by a group of officials and merchants operating in Bermuda. The scheme was a secret one, presumably unknown to the royal government in London. Under its provisions, Tew was granted a privateer's commission by Bermuda authorities. He was sent out not only to seek French ships and to raid French locations, but also, far more importantly, to sail into the Indian Ocean and the Red Sea in search of treasure ships belonging to the Great Mogul. It was on this mission that Captain Tew set sail from Bermuda in December 1692 in the seventy-ton sloop, *Amity*.

In carrying out this mission, Tew was a much-heralded success. In April 1693, he attacked a huge treasure ship and rather easily captured its cargo of silks, ivory, spices, gold, and silver. A year later, Tew and *Amity*, after a refitting on the island of Madagascar, sailed into Newport harbor much to the delight of that city's merchants and consumers.

The success of this voyage, which in the view of many historians opened the Golden Age of piracy because of the new treasure potential that now beckoned in the waters of Asia, was unfortunately a siren song for Tew. He set sail again to attack the Great Mogul's ships but, in September 1695, he was killed aboard the *Amity* during an attempted assault.[22]

Finally, one cannot omit Henry Morgan from the list. Born in Wales, Morgan was an early privateer who took his position most seriously. In what would be recorded as one of the most ferocious attacks in history, Morgan raided Panama in 1671. He burned and looted churches; destroyed forts, warehouses, and homes; and generally raped and murdered his way through the town in search of gold or anything else of value.

The Spanish labeled Morgan a pirate but the English government honored him with a knighthood and later named him lieutenant governor of Jamaica.[23]

THE PARDONS AND THE END

One of the things that made piracy attractive in the Golden Age was that most pirates were not brought to justice. Many, particularly the members of pirate crews, were usually able to make a successful case that they had been forced into their actions. While this statement was usually untrue it was often accepted. Additionally, many pirate captains escaped punishment because the government (usually that of Great Britain) was convinced that they had performed a valuable service to the Crown. However, the argument had virtually no weight if piracy was conducted against an English ship.

Many of the pirates, Morgan being only one, stole so much that they ended their lives peacefully as rich men who beat the system. They are among the not inconsiderable group in history to which the old adage "crime does not pay" brings forth a cynical snicker.

In 1718, Woodes Rogers, a British naval officer and the governor general of the Bahamas, backed by significant military support (including former pirates) on New Providence, offered pardons to those engaged in piracy.

While it is true that some of those who accepted the royal pardons returned to their plundering ways, most of the approximately two thousand who accepted the offer did not. The back of piracy was effectively broken.

The pardons, of course, were not the only factor that caused the demise of the Golden Age of piracy. The ability of naval forces to control piracy was increasing; the number of merchant ships that could be seized was becoming more limited as they carried less treasure and even more guns. And, surely not to be ignored, it was becoming more difficult to find merchants who would double as fences in the major port cities. The risks for them, too, had grown beyond the level of acceptability.

The clock had run out on the Golden Age of pirates.

THE "MODERN" AGE

Piracy did not die when its Golden Age ended. Naval campaigns were mounted against it by most of the major seafaring nations including the United States, into the middle of the nineteenth century.[24]

The waters of Southeast Asia, to include the Straits of Malacca, the Philippine Sea, and the South China Sea, have never been free of the piracy scourge. Only World War II provided relief from pirates and they returned to the waters of the area immediately after the conflict ended. In recent years, piracy has increased not only in Southeast Asia but also around the world and with particular ferocity off the coasts and in the harbors of both Africa and South America.

There is another part of this crime and one where the cost cannot be truly determined except in terms of medical expenses and accompanying lost time—calculations that belong in the realm of the number crunchers. The real cost, in human terms, is found in the sheer numbers of wounded and murdered people as well as in the trauma sustained (and often carried for life) by the surviving victims of pirate attacks.

Any examination of the activities of modern-day pirates and their increasing propensity to bloody violence leads to one inescapable conclusion and associated solution. Pirates, wherever they conduct their dirty trade, are criminals. Like all criminals, their behavior can range from the petty to the most felonious. By no measure can pirates and piracy be considered as merely some kind of seaborne annoyance.

Pirates, as has been known from the first days of maritime crime, richly deserve punishment ranging from imprisonment to execution. As illustrated by some of their comments contained in this chapter, they are proud of their endeavors and culture. They must be made to understand that there is a price to be paid for it either in summary fashion when running afoul of some naval or law enforcement agency or, less dramatically, at the hands of a criminal court.

PIRATES AND THEIR BLOODY CULTURE

The following account is provided by a modern-day piracy victim.

> I was roused at 0330 hours at the sound of rapid blasts on the ship whistle, followed by a phone call from the watchkeeper to say we had intruders on board on the foredeck, I went immediately to the bridge and was advised by the second officer that gunshots had been heard and he believed (that) the chief officer had been hit.[25]

Except for the modern wording of the above recital the incident would seem to belong to a page in a logbook from the early 1700s. Most people would not believe that the entry was written only about a decade ago.

Modern pirates do not fit the Errol Flynn or Douglas Fairbanks images of Hollywood fame and glory. Instead, they are bloodthirsty slime creatures who inhabit the port areas and waterways of much of the underdeveloped and newly developing areas of the world. Their rocket launchers, bolo knives, and automatic weapons are real and used with little, if any, provocation.

Piracy occurs today in many parts of the world and although all nations have agreed to discourage and punish it, pirate acts are on the rise with every passing year and at an alarming rate. Unfortunately, it is probably true that as long as there is waterborne trade, pirates will be lurking in the shadows. Despite the fact that innocent merchant crew members are themselves attacked when pirates strike, it is also true and far more unfortunate that little is being done to stop it. There is, sadly, no real monetary profit to be gained in stopping piracy attacks on people, a fact coupled with another—Americans and others around the world simply do not recognize that piracy really exists as a modern menace. The truth sometimes comes into focus stained with human blood.

In 1980, one member of the House of Representatives was sailing off the Bahamas near Pipe Cay when he and his son sighted a yacht that was adrift. A closer examination revealed the body of a man draped over the gunwales, a seat cushion caked with dried blood, a quantity of spent cartridges on deck, and numerous holes in the hull, presumably made by a shotgun. Cash that had been on the boat and the owner's firearms were missing.

This incident, an attack on the high seas, flies directly in the face of the previously mentioned belief that the crime of piracy disappeared into the mists of history.

Most modern pirates are well armed and highly organized, and employ significant planning.[26] Much like their predecessors, they attack targets that they consider to be generally unprepared.

There should be no mistake about the fact that pirates are still plying the seas (and some harbors—with emphasis on the ports of Brazil) and that the numbers of pirate strikes and the ferocity that mark them are increasing at an alarming rate.

A 1986 publication of the International Chamber of Commerce chronicled over three hundred incidents of piracy in the period from 1961 through 1986. By comparison, a 1989 edition of the same publication noted over seven hundred incidents from 1981 through 1987. These numbers do not include attacks against boat people that take place in the waters of Southeast Asia. In Thailand alone from 1981 through 1988, there were almost one thousand such documented attacks. Overall, pirate attacks during the last decade have resulted in hundreds of deaths and injuries plus thefts of stolen property measured in the millions of dollars. Refugees have been attacked, yachts have been seized and looted, crew members and ship passengers have been murdered, and numerous kidnappings have occurred for the purpose of collecting ransom money.

The danger posed by pirates is acutely felt by seafarers whether on commercial ships, sampans in the South China Sea, fishing boats in the Caribbean, or pleasure craft. Whether items stolen are a vessel's equipment or its cargo, mariners themselves are almost always among the targets of pirate attacks.

It is reasonable for seafarers to expect to sail seas that are safe from pirates and thus the trauma of a piracy attack can leave a mariner scarred for life both physically and emotionally. Fear, coupled with a feeling of impending, but unpredictable, doom is felt by all who are attacked by pirates. A Filipino seafarer wrote about his experience as the victim of a pirate attack.

I quickly jumped out of bed and opened the door. I was astounded to see two strangers, faces covered with handkerchiefs, each with a handgun, a .38 revolver and a .45 automatic, poked right into my face. How were they able to come on board? We were attacked by a group of armed men who unbelievably came onboard unnoticed while the ship was running at full speed.[27]

THE PIRATE "CODE"

One pirate recently told a reporter: "We have a special torture for prisoners. We hang them on a branch by their feet and burn them alive. Then we eat their ears."[28] Another one said, "To kill is to eat. My rifle is my life. I despise my victims. Every time I attack, I feel like chopping their guts out."[29]

No matter how seriously these pirate statements are taken there is no question, if one is to accept the reports provided by the International Maritime Bureau (IMB), that violence during the course of pirate attacks is on the rise.

There seems to be one primary cause for the sharp rise in pirate activity, namely the general downturn in the international economy. The secretary general of the International Maritime Organization has warned the maritime community to exercise extra levels of vigilance because of that fact. It has been assumed that economic problems in several regions of the globe could increase the propensity for piracy—particularly where it has been historically endemic.

MURDER AT SEA

Seafarers face many different types of threat from pirates. The most fearsome, of course, is bodily harm. One handwritten message given by pirates to the captain of the *Baltimar Zephyr* just before he was shot to death was: "I need your all money if you do not like hurt no speak follow order also you take crew money [*sic*]."[30]

In that incident both the captain and the first officer were murdered, and the pirates then emptied the ship's safe, taking several hundred dollars. Three other seafarers were thrown overboard. The pirates then left the ship as it plowed unpiloted through the night for miles before the few crew members left aboard finally regained control.

Crew members are not the only people at risk. The highly publicized attack on the cruise ship *Achille Lauro* in 1985 resulted in the murder of an American passenger, Leon Klinghoffer. It should be noted that the killers in that case were not considered pirates under the law but terrorists because their principal motivation was political. It is a definition that seems strained and, as noted in chapter 2, may be in the process of change.

TERROR AND LOSS

Mariners, by necessity, live where they work. When pirates board a ship they are invading not only the seafarers' workplace, but their homes as well. Although a May 1998 attack in Indian waters on the liquid petroleum gas tanker *World Sky* resulted merely in the loss of some of the ship's equipment, the crew who discovered the pirate intruders also (and quite justifiably) felt violated, helpless, and unsafe. The same was true of the crew of the *Nelvana,* which was attacked in September 1998 in Jamaica, another case where the ship's equipment was stolen.

On 9 March 1998, the *Gebruder Winter* was attacked off Brazil by a band of armed pirates who locked up the crew and ransacked the rest of the ship. The master was beaten and forced to open the ship's safe, the contents of which were then stolen along with items from various containers aboard the vessel.[31]

Because a ship must serve as a crew member's home for several months at a time, individuals frequently bring with them items of high sentimental value as well as other personal items. When the *Cape Sable* was attacked by pirates off Hong Kong in April 1997, one crew member was stabbed when he resisted their stealing over $17,000 in crew wages, a laptop computer, a video camera, and other electronic equipment. In an attack on the *Leira* in July 1997 off Indonesia, the master and chief officer were tied up and robbed of cash and personal items. Such losses leave seafarers devastated. Life away from home is hard enough. The loss of items such as wedding bands, wristwatches, and other jewelry and personal goods can make life at sea almost intolerable.

Sometimes, even when pirates are captured by authorities, the seafarers on board become victims twice, once from pirates and then from the law enforcement authorities. According to reports on the hijacking of the *Petro Ranger* in April 1998, Chinese police held the Australian master and twenty members of the crew prisoner aboard the ship for two weeks *after* being freed from Indonesian pirates who had taken over the vessel. While detained, the master and crew were forbidden to have any contact with the outside world.

As an aside, and indicative of the continuing and repetitive dangers faced today, the *Petro Ranger,* according to IMB reports, had been attacked by pirates in November 1997. In that incident, the pirates were repulsed.

The crew of the ill-fated *Virgin Pearl* was far less fortunate than the mariners of the *Petro Ranger.* In April 1998, the *Virgin Pearl* disappeared while returning from its maiden voyage to Indonesia.[32] On 4 April, the Philippine Coast Guard received a report that the ship was sinking but that its crew of fifteen (along with nine passengers) had been rescued by a Japanese merchant vessel.

The first sign that something was wrong came when a check of the Japanese ship's name showed that no such vessel existed. Later, the bodies of two crew members were found floating in waters off Malaysia. The victims, according to official reports, had been severely mistreated before they were murdered.

Several months passed with no further word regarding either the *Virgin Pearl* or any possibly remaining survivors. In August, the owner of the ship received word from an individual referred to only as a "pirate emissary" that the twenty-two survivors were alive and well and being held captive in Sabah, Malaysia. Not without surprise, a ransom of one million pesos—the equivalent of $24,000—was demanded. Subsequently, two unsuccessful attempts were made to rescue the victims. As of this writing, the fate of these victims remains a mystery.

A NEED FOR SOLUTIONS

While it may be true that the economic losses sustained by shipowners; by merchants who use the ships; and by the insurance companies who provide coverage for hulls and cargoes, have not reached high enough levels to generate much interest in the piracy problem—the costs in human terms have already done so and the price could go much higher.

Again, we can estimate the numbers of personal injuries, deaths, and cases of psychological trauma sustained by those who serve aboard merchant ships and we can do so with some good degree of accuracy. By contrast, the number of fishermen, boat people, and others who fall victim to pirates is far more difficult to calculate.

The time has long since arrived when pirates and terrorists must be made to pay for their crimes and in a manner that will, to use a very popular (although overly used and often meaningless) phrase, send a message. However that message is conveyed it must be one that cannot be misunderstood by the marine miscreants who prowl the oceans, harbors, and rivers of the world.

Pirates and the Law

The so-called law of piracy is a curious mix of international and national law. It is often difficult to explain to the nonlawyer why a particular crime or act of deprivation may not squarely fall within the legal definition of piracy. Furthermore, to define what the law of piracy or the legal response to piracy has been, it is essential to first understand how broad the definition of the term "legal" may be.

While it is true that many offending pirates have had their necks stretched (or worse) after capture, there are many who have been befriended and perhaps nurtured by nations based upon national interest. It is interesting to note that although piracy has existed in some form or another since the institution of maritime commerce during the crusades, the accepted international definition of the law of piracy dates only to 1958.

Piracy has been described as a crime against nations or an international crime, yet the internationally accepted definition of piracy limits itself to crimes against private individuals and private property (including vessels and aircraft). Many adults may remember newsworthy incidents in the past twenty to thirty years such as the *Mayaguez* and *Achille Lauro* incidents, and other such notorious events that certainly seemed like piratical acts. The term "piracy" has even been extended to the nonmaritime vernacular to include the theft of software and other types of intellectual property. Unfortunately, the use of the term in modern American dialogue goes far beyond the legal definition of piracy. This is largely due to the misuse and abuse of the term by those who want to stamp a particular act with a well-known and attention-getting epithet.

To understand what the law (or the legal definition) of piracy is, one needs to first have "a feel for the game" in terms of what the words "law" or "legal" entail.

The words "law" and "legal" in Western civilization generally refer to a set of guidelines or norms that govern the conduct of persons in civilized/socialized groups. The underlying basis of law may fall into two categories—statutory law and common law.

In the United States, the definition of statutory law is quite simple. Statutory laws are the laws enacted by federal, state, and local governments comprised of elected representatives. By contrast, common law is not found in statutes or regulations, but rather it is law that has been handed down through the ages by judicial interpretation of what rules or norms should govern civilized society. An example of common law versus statutory law is that in the United States there are normally no state or federal statutes requiring that you compensate your neighbors for accidental damage that you do to their property. The common law, however, would require that you reimburse a neighbor for such damage whether it was caused by negligence or by an intentional act.

The problem with defining piracy on an international basis is that most piratical acts occur upon the high seas and beyond the bounds of national jurisdiction. If an act of piracy occurs within the territorial jurisdiction of the nation-state, the act may be punishable by laws that do not use the word "piracy." Those criminal laws may include such terms as larceny, robbery, murder, kidnapping, battery, and the like. Therein lies the rub. Should an act of piracy occur within the territorial jurisdiction of a nation and if the offenders are apprehended, the action will be prosecuted as something other than piracy. Only acts that do not occur within the territorial jurisdiction of a nation are truly termed piracy.

Public international law, in contrast to national law, has a broader range of sources. While they are the same basic ones, that is, statutory and common law, others also exist. In the public international law context, the sources of statutory law include treaties and international conventions. Common law sources include decisions of properly constituted international law tribunals such as the International Court of Justice or its predecessor, the Permanent International Court of Justice, at The Hague. In addition, other accepted sources of international law that govern the relations between and among the nations include the writings of international publicists, custom and usage in the relations between and among nations, as well as the doctrine of comity. The doctrine of comity provides that one nation as an accommodation to another will allow the enforcement of another nation's laws in its own courts.

Although piracy in the most traditional form had its Golden Age come and go in the seventeenth and early-eighteenth centuries, piracy was not really defined as a crime by international treaty until 1958. As a result of that definition, many acts of maritime deprivation that the layman might consider piracy do not fall squarely within the legal definition of piracy.

There were, of course, earlier common law and statutory definitions that were accepted at the national level well before the current international definition was codified. For example, Sir Charles Hedges, a "Judge of the Admiralty," gave the following definition of piracy in a 1696 trial at the Old Bailey in London:

> Now piracy is only a term for sea-robbery, piracy being committed within the jurisdiction of the Admiralty. If any man shall be assaulted within that jurisdiction, and his ship or goods violently taken away without legal authority, this is robbery and piracy. If the mariners of any ship shall violently dispossess the master, and afterwards carry away the ship itself or any of the goods, or tackle, apparel or furniture, in any place where the Lord Admiral hath, or pretends to have jurisdiction, this is also robbery and piracy.[1]

Pirates have been around as long as there has been maritime commerce. It is a little known fact that present-day commercial law has its roots in some of the original maritime codes. Those codes, which serve in part as a basis for modern admiralty law, set forth rules and responsibilities to govern maritime commercial activities (including piracy) as early as 500 B.C., and governed the Mediterranean Sea from 300 B.C. until 1200 A.D. They were followed and supplemented by other well-known codes including the Rules of Oleron, the Consolata Del Mar, the Rules of Visby, and those of the Hanseatic League. Indeed, until almost the end of the eighteenth century, maritime legal matters, including criminal cases, were handled by specially constituted admiralty courts.[2]

In 1958, the international community put together four separate international treaties or conventions governing the law of the sea. They were respectively the 1958 Geneva Conventions on the Territorial Sea and Contiguous Zone, the Continental Shelf, the High Seas, and Fisheries. Only one of those treaties is important to this discussion regarding the legal definition of piracy, the 1958 Geneva Convention on the High Seas. Article 15 of the Convention sets forth the definition of piracy as follows:

Piracy consists of any of the following acts:

1. Any illegal acts of violence, terrorism, or any act of depredation committed for private ends by the crew or the passengers of a private ship or private aircraft, and directed at,

a. on the high seas, against the ship or aircraft, or against persons or property on board such ship or aircraft;

b. against a ship, aircraft, persons, or property in a place outside the jurisdiction of any State;

2. Any act of voluntary participation in the operation of a ship or of an aircraft with knowledge of facts making it a pirate ship or aircraft;

3. Any act of inciting or intentionally facilitating an act described in Paragraph 1 above or Subparagraph 2 of this article.[3]

Upon review of the above, there are two major exceptions to the legal international definition of piracy. The first is that the act itself must take place on the high seas or beyond the jurisdiction of any nation.

The reason for this exception is that in order for an act to be a crime against nations, it must occur beyond the jurisdiction of any particular nation. The right to enforce law by any nation's law enforcement authorities is limited to that state's territorial jurisdiction. In other words, one nation may not send its law-enforcement authorities into another nation's territorial jurisdiction to enforce either national or international law.

Prior to the early 1980s, the coastal state jurisdiction of the adjacent seas extended from the low-water mark on the beach to a distance of three nautical miles seaward (a nautical mile is two thousand yards). This area encompassed what is commonly known as the territorial sea. The territorial sea has expanded to twelve nautical miles since the mid-1980s. However, prior to 1982 many nations claimed a wider breadth of the territorial sea from twelve to two hundred nautical miles. The three-mile rule as the limit of national jurisdiction over the seas has two separate but equally believable underpinnings. The first is that a person measuring five feet to five-and-a-half feet tall standing on the beach would be able to see approximately three nautical miles or six thousand yards distant to the horizon. Thus, if the king owned all the king could see, the king could see three miles to sea and owned that territory. The second theory is that the average distance that a cannonball would fly after being fired from a battery or fort would be approximately six thousand yards or three nautical miles.[4]

Within the territorial sea, a coastal state may exercise complete dominion and control and has the exclusive prerogative to enforce its laws.[5]

In 1958, a second and lesser concept of jurisdiction over the seas, which noticed a contiguous zone, was officially sanctioned by the international community.[6] The contiguous zone began at the seaward edge of the territorial sea (or three miles) and extended an additional nine miles seaward (to twelve miles). Within the contiguous zone, nations were allowed to a lesser degree to enforce laws, which were limited to customs, fiscal, and sanitary laws. While piracy does not necessarily fall within the definition of customs, fiscal, and sanitary laws, it is nevertheless a crime that could be responded to by a nation within the contiguous zone.

In addition to the jurisdiction over the specific geographic bodies of water, such as the territorial sea and the contiguous zone, nations also have jurisdiction over vessels that are registered under their laws, or, in the vernacular, "fly their flag." Thus, if an incident occurs on a vessel that is flagged under U.S. law (i.e., documented with the United States Coast Guard), the United States has authority to enforce its laws aboard that vessel or otherwise prosecute individuals for crimes that occur aboard it regardless of the ship's location at the time of the incident. For example, if a robbery and murder occur aboard a U.S.-flagged vessel one mile off the coast of Marseilles, France, the French authorities might have territorial jurisdiction due to the location of the incident but the United States would also have jurisdiction to punish the offenders because the vessel is considered U.S. territory.

This first exception to the modern international definition of piracy has been solved in one way or another by the fact that most nations have closed the gap by enacting national laws that provide for the punishment of piratical acts within their national jurisdiction. In the United States, federal law provides for the punishment of piracy by life imprisonment. Piracy is defined under U.S. law as follows:

1. Any act of piracy as defined by international law if the perpetrators are found in the United States.

2. Any act of murder, robbery, or hostility against the United States or against a United States citizen on the high seas, by a citizen of the United States.

3. Acts by aliens against the United States or its citizens that are defined as piracy in the treaty between the nation that the individual is a citizen of and the United States.[7]

Beyond this limited definition of piracy in the United States, federal or state law may set forth statutes and regulations that would otherwise punish piratical acts under a separate name such as robbery, murder, larceny, or kidnapping. These statutes do not evoke the romanticism and notions of salt air, gunpowder, rum, and gold coins; but they do provide a legal basis for the prosecution of pirates and the like when they act within U.S. territory. Indeed, depending on the locus of the act, the crime committed by pirates, be it robbery, larceny, murder, or kidnapping, may have a stiffer penalty depending upon whether it is prosecuted under state or federal law.

A second major exception to the legal definition of piracy that distinguishes it from terrorism is that the particular act must have been committed for "private ends" in order for it to be piracy. In essence, that part of the legal definition means that actions against vessels on the high seas or against aircraft in international skies are not piracy if at the time the underlying motive is political in nature, whether or not sanctioned by a recognized government.

In 1961, the Portuguese cruise vessel *Santa Maria* was reported to have been attacked by pirates in the Caribbean. Immediate requests for assistance went out to all Caribbean nations and to the United States.

The U.S. Navy apparently began a search for the vessel while at the same time the lawyers at the U.S. State Department began to investigate the facts. Before the Navy found the *Santa Maria,* the lawyers and diplomats had concluded that no act of piracy had taken place.

Indeed, the investigation revealed that one Captain Galvano and his compatriots peaceably boarded the *Santa Maria* while in port. There was no involvement of a second vessel that could be termed a pirate ship. Moreover, the so-called pirates were Portuguese revolutionaries seeking to make a political statement on the eve of a possible insurrection in Portugal. Accordingly, the search was shut down by the U.S. Navy, as there was no clear indication of a "piratical act."[8]

This particular incident led one commentator to suggest as early as 1972 that the legal definition of piracy under international conventions be modified to change the phrase "for private gain" to "without authority." (Presumably, the "without authority" wording meant lack of sanction by recognized national or international authority.)[9]

It is interesting to note that despite the *Santa Maria* incident and other acts such as airplane hijackings during the 1960s and 1970s, the international community failed to take any opportunity to amend the definition of piracy. In the mid-70s, the Third United Nations Conference on the Law of the Sea was convened. The conference went through eight negotiating sessions and dealt with many issues regarding the breadth of the territorial sea, deep-seabed mining, and extended national jurisdiction over the seas. The negotiating sessions lasted almost nine years. Through the negotiating sessions and the reports of the negotiating sessions, there appears to have been little or no concern about revising the definition of piracy.[10] Indeed, when the Third United Nations Conference on the Law of the Sea was put into its final form, the definition of piracy mirrored the definition in the 1958 Geneva Convention on the High Seas.[11]

Unfortunately, lightning struck again just as the Law of the Sea Convention was being ratified. In 1985, as mentioned earlier, the Italian cruise ship *Achille Lauro* was taken over by elements of the Palestine Liberation Organization (PLO). The *Achille Lauro* incident provides an interesting example of current-day responses to piracy and the continued problem with defining it.

During the course of the incident in which one American passenger was murdered, the four hijackers were said to be in contact with members of the parent PLO. Eventually, a deal was brokered that allowed for safe passage of the hijackers into Egypt. Despite the gravity of what the four had accomplished aboard the *Achille Lauro,* the Egyptian government, for political reasons, refused to detain, try, or extradite the four Palestinians. Egypt did, however, provide the hijackers with a flight out of the country that was intercepted by U.S. Navy fighter aircraft and forced to land at a NATO base in Italy. The Italian government took custody of the four.

The United States issued an arrest warrant for the hijackers for hostage taking under the Comprehensive Crime Control Act of 1984; piracy under 18USC, sub. sec. 1651; and conspiracy. A charge of murder was not included in the warrant because there was no law making the murder of a citizen beyond U.S. jurisdiction a crime.[12]

The arrest warrant, for all the vigor that accompanied its issuance, soon became moot. The Italian government quite properly refused to extradite the Palestinians for two reasons. First, Italy wanted to prosecute the criminals in its own courts. Second, treaties and conventions that were then in force did not require Italy to extradite the criminals to a nation that maintained a death penalty. The Palestinians were convicted of murder and hijacking by Italy in 1986.

The *Achille Lauro* incident, much like the *Santa Maria* incident some twenty years before, did not constitute piracy, as only a single vessel was involved, and the underlying motive was not for private gain but rather for political or quasi-political purposes. This is despite the fact that both President Ronald Reagan and a sitting federal judge referred to the incident as an act of piracy.[13]

Despite many commentators calling for a revised definition of piracy, nothing has changed. Indeed, some authorities have suggested that the definition of piracy should be merged with the definition of terrorism. Others, by contrast, have taken the position that although there is a fixed definition of piracy in the two relevant conventions, the customary international law may supplement statutory law that is found in treaties and in international conventions and must evolve to take into account the development and needs of international society. One would argue that although events such as the *Achille Lauro* and the *Santa Maria* do not squarely fit within the written definition of piracy, they are nonetheless piratical acts and should be punished as the same. This is the same way American common law developed during this past century to create new theories such as products liability.[14] Others have again suggested a change in the definition of piracy.[15] Perhaps an expansion of the common law definition is most appropriate, as it is obvious that most reasonable people would consider the *Achille Lauro* incident to be one of piracy despite the statutory definition. This somewhat calls to mind a statement by a well-known U.S. Supreme Court justice who was asked to define pornography. The response to the question was that he could not define it but he certainly knew it when he saw it.

The legal definition of terrorism is much less problematical. There are four international conventions dealing with terrorism: (1) The Hague Convention on the Suppression of Unlawful Seizure of Aircraft (12/16/70, 22UST1641, 860 UNTS 105); (2) The Convention for the Suppression of Unlawful Acts Against the Safety of Civil Aviation (9/23/71, 24UST564 [Montreal Convention]); (3) The Convention Against the Taking of Hostages (12/17/79, 18ILM1456 [1979]); and (4) The Convention on the Preservation and Punishment of Crimes Against Internationally Protected Persons Including Diplomatic Agents (12/14/73, 28UST1975). As a result of the *Achille Lauro* hijacking, Italy proposed a convention to the International Maritime Organization entitled "Convention for the Suppression of Unlawful Acts Against the Safety of Maritime Navigation."

Significantly this convention deals not only with the suppression of maritime terrorism, but also with the apprehension, conviction, and punishment of those who commit maritime terrorism. The convention contains an "extradite or prosecute" requirement.[16]

Despite the problems with the definition of piracy, the legal response to piracy over the last two hundred years has been a mixed bag. The legal response does not mean that pirates must be arrested, indicted, tried, and convicted. The term "legal response" encompasses all possible responses that a properly constituted nation of laws and its citizens may do either publicly or privately to react to a particular situation. A legal response may thus involve political and military responses as well as courtroom proceedings. Indeed, the courtroom proceedings may be criminal or civil in nature.

There is an interesting footnote to the legal response in the *Achille Lauro* incident that is reminiscent of advice about maintaining discipline aboard ships. An old salt once stated, "When a sailor gets out of line, hitting him in the head does little good, but if you hit him in the wallet you will see a changed man."[17] The family of Leon Klinghoffer did just that and perhaps will impose a sanction against the PLO more significant than some of the diplomatic attempts. The Klinghoffer family filed a wrongful death suit in the U.S. District Court for the Southern District of New York after the *Achille Lauro* incident. The defendants in the suit included Achille Lauro Cruise Lines and, eventually, the Palestine Liberation Organization. Initially, an attempt was made to attach the assets of the PLO in New York, including property that provided residence and offices for their appointed delegation to the United Nations. Despite the fact that the PLO put forward several procedural obstacles, the court found that the PLO was a nonrecognized nation at the time of the incident and was not entitled to sovereign immunity.

Also, the court said, whatever international treaties or U.S. criminal statutes might have applied to the murder of Klinghoffer, that death occurred on or over the navigable waters, was wrongful in nature, and thereby constituted a maritime tort (much the same as if Klinghoffer's death had occurred due to some negligence of the crew of the vessel). Despite several obstacles and procedural decisions, Judge Louis L. Stanton initially determined that the PLO was susceptible to being held liable for monetary damages by the estate of Mr. Klinghoffer.[18]

As discussed above, the legal response to piracy or terrorism has always taken the path of apprehension, prosecution, and punishment of pirates or terrorists. While piracy remains ill defined, terrorism has become broadly and adequately defined in the last forty years. In the heyday of pirates, however, the response to piracy was somewhat different.

THE OLD DAYS

What constitutes a pirate? Does it mean merely that one has to ravage and plunder unsuspecting merchant vessels or simply be part of a pirate ship crew? An interesting example of somebody who was found not to be a pirate although facilitated piratical acts was that of Thomas Davis, a carpenter aboard the pirate ship *Whydah*. The *Whydah* had been commissioned as a merchant slave ship and was named for the port of Ouida on the West African slave coast. The pirate Black Belamy seized the *Whydah* in the early 1700s. Thomas Davis, a Welshman, was brought aboard the *Whydah* after Belamy and his crew captured the *St. Michael,* on which Davis had served. Davis had requested that his life be spared and as a result became the ship's carpenter.

Belamy and the crew of the *Whydah,* as well as associated ships, ravaged the east coast of the United States and the Caribbean as pirates during 1716. The *Whydah* eventually foundered off the coast of Cape Cod. Davis was one of a very few members of the some 180 people in the *Whydah*'s crew that made it ashore safely, despite the worst elements. In addition, members of the pirate crew on the *Fisher,* also within Belamy's flotilla, arrived ashore in Cape Cod shortly after the *Whydah*'s demise in early 1717. All of the "gentlemen" were taken into custody by local authorities and were later transferred to a prison in Boston.

In 1717, twelve judges of the Judiciary Court of Admiralty (sanctioned by the Crown) were assembled in the Boston Courthouse. The twelve judges included Governor Schute and Lt. Gov. William Dummer. It took little time for the court to find that Davis's involvement with the *Whydah* was not an act of piracy, as he had been forced to stay against his will. Indeed, Davis was defended by Cotton Mather, a Puritan cleric and statesman. Davis's compatriots from the other pirate vessels did not fare so well. They were convicted by the same Admiralty Court, and were eventually hanged in Charlestown, Massachusetts.[19]

Despite the way in which the other pirates aboard the *Whydah* shuffled off their mortal coils, the legal response to piracy in Massachusetts in the early 1700s was not completely altruistic. At the time of the *Whydah*'s foundering, Samuel Schute was a colonial governor. British law gave abandoned pirate and perhaps other property found on the sea to the Crown. It is noted in a recent treatise regarding the *Whydah* that Schute had every reason to believe that the Crown might reward him personally if the *Whydah*'s treasure were recovered from the vessel and sent to the king.[20] Unfortunately, many of the inhabitants of Cape Cod already had the same idea and had gone about salvaging and collecting any bits of treasure or other articles of value from the wreck. Undaunted by the simple fact of business as usual along the New England coast, Governor Schute commissioned Capt. Cyprian Southhack to examine the wreck as well as go door-to-door along Cape Cod and recover the Crown's property. Artifacts from the pirate ship *Whydah* as well as some of its history now reside in the Pirate Museum in Provincetown, Massachusetts.

Later in the eighteenth century the legal response of the fledgling United States to piracy was somewhat different. Before the United States became independent, it had benefited from the protection of the British naval forces with regard to piracy. Upon independence, America as a small maritime nation found itself having to fend for itself. One of the primary issues that confronted the U.S. maritime commerce was that of the Barbary States along the coast of North Africa.

It has often been said that the Barbary pirates, as they have been since termed, resulted in the birth of the U.S. Navy in the 1790s. The initial response of the United States was to pay tribute to the pirates so that American-flagged vessels might pass through their area of operations without attack or other interruption. The treaties with the Barbary States lasted for several years but eventually the potentates became anxious to break them as the value of American commerce that they might plunder was much greater than what they could gain abiding by the treaties and accepting tribute.

Provoked by treaty violations, in 1805 the United States engaged the Barbary pirates in warfare that lasted for ten years. It was not until March 1815 that Comdr. Steven Decatur, as commander of a naval squadron sent to the Mediterranean, finally put an end to the pirates' ravaging and blackmail by a show of naval force. At that juncture, the payment of tribute to the pirates ended along with America's trouble with the Barbary States of North Africa.[21]

Even today, the actions of the Barbary pirates would not legally be considered piracy because they were working under the auspices of North African potentates. Since their actions were sanctioned by some sort of recognized government, the actions were not necessarily for private ends.

Perhaps the best evidence of the first response of the fledgling United States to piracy exists to be viewed by the public today. The USS *Constitution* and the USS *Constellation,* two of the frigates commissioned during the 1790s, which formed the nucleus of the U.S. Navy, are still available for public viewing. Indeed, the USS *Constitution* engaged the Barbary pirates under the command of Capt. Edward Preble between 1803 and 1804. The vessel sits today in Boston Harbor, Massachusetts, and may be toured by anyone interested in the history of the vessel. In fact, the other vessels commissioned at the same time as the *Constitution* include the *Philadelphia,* the *Constellation,* the *President,* the *United States,* and the *Essex.* The *Constellation* is available for viewing in Baltimore, Maryland.

Maritime crime in the current day has become more legally complicated, but is nonetheless crime and must be treated as the same. In the present day, piracy under the law not only involves assaying rovers and thieves but also includes more complex issues of fraud and misrepresentation, along with simple theft. Perhaps some of the pirates of the seas were more honest than our current software pirates and thieves, as they made no bones about what they were doing and why they were doing it.

Pirates at Work
Europe and the Americas

Pirates, using both the broad-based and more narrow definitions, operate around the world. During 1997, a record year as far as piracy incidents are concerned, pirate attacks were reported to have occurred in the Mediterranean, off both coasts of South Africa and South America, as well as in the waters of Southeast Asia.

And, of course, there is the Caribbean.

It seems as unforgivable when writing a book about pirates and piracy to ignore the Caribbean as it does to forget about the Jolly Roger. Golden Age pirates, despite their connections to places like far-off Madagascar, are still wedded in history to this ocean and its islands. During the 1970s and 1980s, that connection once again came into focus.

There is absolutely no question that many people and pleasure boats were lost during that period, presumably to drug smugglers, in the Caribbean.[1] But the problem was not limited to that ocean. There were reported (and confirmed) disappearances in the Gulf of Mexico, off Baja California, and in the Pacific, off Hawaii. The disappearance of these boats and the crews aboard them came to be described by a new word in the English language, "yachtjacking."

Some cases involving pleasure craft far away from the Caribbean, which are known to be drug-smuggler related, include the racing yacht *Kamillii* and the trawler-yacht *Lupita.* The *Kamillii* was seized by three armed men in the waters off Hawaii and the crew members were set adrift in a life raft 140 miles at sea. Luckily, a passing freighter saved them. The *Lupita* was found wrecked on an island in the Gulf of California. Law enforcement officials believe that the two American couples who had been onboard were murdered. The killers, probably also Americans and posing as college students needing jobs, were hired by the boat owners at some port. In reality, the "students" were drug runners who killed the couples and used the *Lupita* for one drug run. The boat was then abandoned. Both of these incidents occurred in the early 1970s.[2]

Despite these cases in the Pacific, most of the actual or suspected yachtjackings by drug smugglers occurred in the Caribbean. In the minds of some pleasure boaters, the danger is still there.

FOLKLORE, RUMOR, AND REALITY

It was a blustery day in late March. We were sitting in a midtown Manhattan restaurant and had been discussing this book. My lunch partner was a very experienced pleasure-boat owner and sailor and his words were every bit as chilling as the weather outside: "You don't sleep at night on the Caribbean."

"Okay," I said, sensing that there might be something more to be offered about the perils of pleasure boating and piracy on the waters between Florida and the Caribbean islands, "tell me about the pirates and drug smugglers."

The response was disappointing in terms of finding a good dramatic angle, but it was supportive of my research.

"A lot of boats and people have disappeared."

"Do you have any personal knowledge about any of these people and their boats?"

"No."

"How do you know about them?"

"It's all around. You hear about it all the time."

The fact is that while some boats and people disappeared and that a good percentage of them were victims of drug smugglers during the 1970s and 1980s there was never really any widespread pattern of such criminal activity, according to both the Drug Enforcement Agency (DEA) and the U.S. Coast Guard.[3]

If you were a boater in those waters during that period, the question of whether there was a "widespread pattern" or not was, of course, a moot one. There were justifiable fears and not unexpected reactions. People began to collect weapons on their boats including magnum handguns and stainless steel, double-barreled, twelve-gauge shotguns, and to consider the defensive capabilities of flare guns.

In his best-selling novel *Clear and Present Danger,* Tom Clancy tells about the story of a group of pirates who seized control of a yacht, and raped and murdered the owners, as part of a retribution by a Colombian drug cartel.[4] Although a fictional account, and one in which the U.S. Coast Guard catches the perpetrators, both the reality and myth of such incidents caused pleasure boaters to be extra vigilant.

One incident bearing on the two points of suspicion and armed reaction was related to me by an official source whom I considered to be unimpeachable. In the summer of 1977, a group of naval ROTC cadets left a Texas port for a training cruise. The crew was authorized to check out automatic weapons from a naval reserve center, a routine action given the reports of drug smuggler activity in the Gulf of Mexico.

At some point in the cruise, the cadets saw a "blip" on the radar screen that appeared to be shadowing their craft. At about midnight, when the vessel hove to, the "blip" also stopped moving. About one hour later, it began to approach the cadets at high speed.

According to my source, one method of boat seizure that was used (although rarely) by drug smugglers was to attack a boat late at night when the crew was, presumably, asleep and the craft was at anchor. This crew, of course, was operating around the clock and when the "blip" moved toward them, their suspicions were aroused.

A decision was made to determine, in an admittedly unsophisticated manner, if the oncoming craft were a friend or a foe. The senior cadet aboard, noting that the "blip" was approaching from the port side, authorized a brief automatic weapons firing to starboard.

The story goes that immediately upon taking that action, the "blip" turned quickly away. No subsequent radio traffic indicated that another boat had observed or heard the firing and no Coast Guard, Navy, or law enforcement vessel attempted to investigate the situation. This would tend to show that somebody was either too frightened to report the incident or, possibly, had reason not to tell anyone about it.

THE METHODS OF YACHTJACKERS

In most cases, direct boat-to-boat attack was not the way used by yachtjacking drug smugglers to seize a vessel, although boaters were warned by the Coast Guard not to respond to distress calls without checking with them first to determine the legitimacy of the emergency.[5] In fact, it was boat owner and operator carelessness that was the principal reason for trouble on the waters—trouble that could have been easily avoided on land.

Time and time again, boat operators—for whatever reasons—hired crew members who were completely unknown to them. Often the people seeking to be hired were young, looked innocent, and many times posed as college students working their way through the islands. This is what happened in the *Lupita* case and probably in scores of others. Minimal (if any) background checks were made, probably under pressure of the moment to get back on the ocean and the naive assumption that nothing bad could happen in such a beautiful, tropical setting.

Once at sea, the newly hired crew members killed their employers and took the boat. If several trips were planned, the vessel was repainted and given new numbers and a new name. Alternatively, if the vessel would be used only once to move drugs into the United States, the smugglers would sometimes sail into a marina and abandon the craft there. Sooner or later, a marina manager would notice that there had been no payment made for the dock. Inquiries would reveal that the boat had been used by drug smugglers who were, in many cases, also murderers. Either way, the boat was unknown to customs, the DEA, or the U.S. Coast Guard as one that was identified with drug trafficking. The absence of the registered owners was often never explained.

In terms of piracy, this was old wine in new bottles. It brings to mind John Avery as just one example of the Golden Age pirates who began their careers through mutiny and murder.

The disappearance of boats and people from the early 1970s to the late 1980s was a serious enough problem to generate a congressional inquiry and to spawn a book by noted author Peter Benchley, entitled *The Island.* In that book, one character, Burred Makepeace, responds to the question of why boats and people were disappearing around the Bahamas islands of Turks and Caicos:

> We have been dangerous for three hundred and fifty years. We have had rumrunners and gunrunners and pirates and poachers and now the drug people. *We* have not changed, the yachtsmen, they have changed. They think this is a playground. Well, they are damned fools. The boats are gone and the people are dead.[6]

In the mid-1970s, the media were filled with reports of hijackings by drug smugglers. The Coast Guard, according to the report of Representative John Murphy (D-NY) to the House Merchant Marine and Fisheries Committee on the Hijacking of U.S. Pleasure Yachts and Cabin Cruisers, had issued a clear warning that declared:

> Yachtsmen planning to set out for a cruise in the waters of the Caribbean, the Gulf of Mexico, the waters along the Baja, California coast and the western coasts of Central America should be aware that his [*sic*] yacht may become a target for a modern day pirate or hijacker, not by way of a boarding by force ala Captain Teach, but by way of stealth and trickery.[7]

The Coast Guard, in 1975, also openly warned of a "possible pattern of boat disappearance" existing in the southwestern Atlantic and the southeastern part of the North Pacific. The numbers of casualties in terms of both boats and people varied widely but ranged as high as two thousand people presumed murdered and 610 vessels lost to smugglers.

The numbers were not the only point on which the authorities disagreed. Contemporary news accounts revealed that the DEA did not believe that yachtjacking was a major factor in boat disappearances while, at the same time, the Coast Guard was issuing dire warnings about widespread patterns of piratical activities to support drug smuggling. By 1980, even the Coast Guard was starting to take the position that yachtjacking was being "blown out of proportion." In October of that year, the new view was that between twenty and twenty-five boats disappeared annually around the Bahamas and that it was possible that some of them had been taken by drug smugglers.[8]

THE CURRENT SCENE

According to the DEA, the U.S. Coast Guard, and the Bahamas Air Sea Rescue Association (BASRA), there have been no recent yachtjackings either suspected or reported, although there have been some disappearances. The last confirmed pirate attack on a pleasure boat in these waters occurred in September 1992 where a man and his wife shot it out with pirates off Little Abaco island, in the Bahamas. While at anchor and at about midnight, at least two pirates, armed with shotguns, attempted to board the couple's forty-foot sailboat. After exchanging shotgun fire with the pirates, the boat's owner was able to cut the anchor and sail away.

A Coast Guard petty officer is quoted by the local newspaper as saying that pirating in the Bahamas and Caribbean "happens all the time. Everybody carries a gun down there . . . there's a whole lot of pirating on the high seas."[9]

INSURANCE

It was suggested by all of these agencies and several of the editors associated with publications that specifically cover pleasure boating, that insurance fraud, in addition to storms, criminal attacks, and accidents, may be a factor in some disappearances, particularly where the owners and crew survive.

Indeed, articles in the March 1998 issue of *Yachting* illustrate two cases of insurance fraud.[10] A third case was related to me as a way of showing how the methods used to cheat insurance companies covering pleasure boats are both many and varied. In this instance, a pleasure boat owner and his wife told the insurance company and the police that pirates had attacked them and set them adrift after the boat was stolen. The insurance company was suspicious and found the boat less than a quarter of a mile away from where the couple was found. It had been sunk in about thirty feet of water and all of the sea cocks were open. The insurance company investigators thought this was a very suspicious thing for yachtjackers or pirates to do, and denied the claim.

CHANGING TIMES

But there are other reasons that pleasure boats are no longer preferred targets of drug smugglers. As one law enforcement source commented, the modern-day drug smugglers are still getting their product into the United States, but most of it is coming in on airplanes or hidden in containers on cargo ships. The drug operators no longer need to take the relatively high risk of being caught at sea in a small boat. Customs can and does search ships, but there are only so many inspectors to do that job. The result is that perhaps only one in ten freighters is really examined. The increased concern over the use of containerships for drug smuggling has been recently noted by the U.S. Department of Transportation.[11]

Another source noted that there is no reason for a drug importer to steal a pleasure boat. They all have enough money to buy one that isn't on anybody's suspect list (also known as a "hot sheet") and sail it to the United States without much risk. The same official buttressed that comment with the point that drug people can walk away from a plane (or container) load of heroin, cocaine, or marijuana that has a street value of a million dollars and is seized by customs, the DEA, or the Coast Guard. Drug people treat that kind of a loss as "the risk of doing business. It comes with the territory."

A NEW PIRACY

Pirates and smugglers do operate, however. Even though moving drugs into the United States on hijacked yachts may no longer provide a means of making a living, smuggling people into places like Florida and Texas, including criminals from Colombia who work for the drug cartels, still offers excellent revenue-producing opportunities. The favored points of departure are reported to be Bimini and Freeport, both in the Bahamas. The smugglers, or at least many of them, still make their homes in the area, one preferred spot being Andros Island.

Of course, in addition to smuggling, there is always the threat of old-fashioned robbery, as the above-reported cases demonstrate.

There are also unconfirmed reports of classic, high-seas piracy with victims whose stories don't make the newspapers. They are fishermen from Cuba, the Bahamas, Haiti, and other Caribbean locations. Their fishing boats are being captured and the catch off-loaded. Sometimes there is accompanying murder and other violence. But there are no statistics and no official reports.

The reason has to do with culture. Much as within the United States, many crime victims often will not report their problem to the police. Instead, the choice is made to handle grievances through self-help or through gang or family reprisal. The whole thing is kept "in the family." The fishermen who are victims of pirates hold to the same belief.

And so there are no known pirates, no officially wanted ones, and no one convicted of the crime.

Benchley's character was right: the Caribbean pirates have been dangerous for 350 years. They still are.

PIRACY IN NORTHERN CLIMES

There are fewer examples of piracy of any kind, using any definition desired of piracy, in northern waters to include those off Japan and the Kurile Islands. The reasons do not include that there are any fewer ships transiting these waters or that, presumably, there are less real or most certainly, fewer potential maritime criminals. It is, instead, because port and onshore security is far better and because the coast guard, police, and naval presence is greater and more effective.

The statement having been made, it must be modified by the caveat that piracy, at least in the broad form, does still occur, even in harbors of the United States.

PIRATES IN FLORIDA

In January 1998, a group of between eight and thirteen armed robbers boarded the *Shandeline,* a freighter docked in Miami. According to news accounts, the boarders pistol-whipped the crew during their search for cash and jewelry.[12]

Apparently someone on the ship was able to call for help and, as the police arrived, four of the robbers jumped into the water. Several other gang members surrendered, and they, it appears, made the right choice. Two of the four who jumped from the ship later washed up on the banks of the Miami River.

The fact that the newspaper characterized these criminals as pirates does help the International Maritime Bureau (IMB) in its efforts to focus public, media, and government attention on the problem of piracy. Additionally, it does help to increase the statistics in terms of the number of piracy incidents. While there may be some criticism of the expanded definition of piracy, the end result might be a reduction in criminal activity that affects the maritime community. If so, the broadened definition has a definite value.

EUROPE

There is a natural tendency to believe that piracy is an activity that occurs mostly in places other than in the waters of Europe and North America. The reports provided by the IMB and others show that while piracy is a greater threat in some areas more than others, it is clearly a worldwide problem.

In early January 1996, a ferry was hijacked in the waters off Trabzon, Turkey. A hostage situation was resolved only after lengthy negotiations between security forces and the pirates decided the issue. There were no injuries.[13] Later that year, the Mediterranean proved to be a dangerous place with three reported piracy incidents.

On 20 August, armed pirates at Scilla, Italy, boarded a pleasure boat, the *Renalo.* Cash and valuables were taken. The ore carrier *Berge Adria,* at anchor in Taranto, Italy, was boarded and some welding equipment was stolen.[14]

But the most violent incident occurred on 27 September when the motor yacht *Carenia,* moored in a cove off the island of Corfu, was boarded by four armed pirates who had pulled alongside the yacht in a speedboat. The yacht owner tried unsuccessfully to defend himself with a shotgun. The pirates overcame his resistance and then searched the vessel for valuables. As Greek police arrived (having heard gunfire from the boat), a firefight ensued in which the boat owner was killed. The pirates escaped.[15]

Piracy in European waters increased in terms of reported incidents during 1997. Information provided by the IMB refers to ten cases, most of them occurring in the Mediterranean Ocean and the Black Sea.

In chronological order, the first reported piracy case occurred on 11 January and actually involved a mutiny aboard a Russian freighter, the *Ivan Chernych.* The incident took place off the Turkish coast.[16]

On 19 February, the scene shifted to the Black Sea port of Poti, Georgia, where pirates boarded a Cypriot freighter, the *Lady Linda.* No injuries were reported, but property was stolen.

In late May, two yachts were reported stolen on the same day, but from widely separated locations. The *Fair Lady* was taken from a marina in Portugal and the *Feeling* was stolen from the port of Workum in the Netherlands. During that same month, the *Sagittarius,* a Greek-owned yacht, was boarded off Albania by pirates who robbed those on the boat.

A minor incident as far as piracy is concerned, but a recorded one nonetheless, occurred at Malta in August where the *Seagull* was bunkering. Two men got aboard and stole credit cards and some valuables. In June, a Japanese fishing ship was fired on by pirates. Two crew members were injured in an incident off the Kurile Islands.

In two of the most remarkable incidents of the year, at least in European waters, two warships were attacked and on the same date, 11 June. In one of these cases, it was reported that a large unidentified ship fired on an Italian Coast Guard cutter. There were no reported injuries in this encounter. In the second incident of that day, an Albanian speedboat opened fire on a Greek Coast Guard ship, which returned fire. The would-be pirates jumped overboard, leaving rifles, ammunition, hand grenades, and a quantity of hashish on their abandoned boat.

SOUTH AMERICA AND CENTRAL AMERICA

While cases of drug-related seizures of pleasure boats have not, as mentioned earlier, been a feature of piracy in Central America for several years, other kinds of piratical activity are of major concern.

At least to date, according to reported incidents noted by the IMB through 31 December 1997, piracy attacks that have occurred in Central and South America have, except for some river actions, taken place in ports and at anchorages, not on the high seas.

During 1996, there were twenty-eight occurrences in this geographic area, with twenty of them taking place in Brazilian waters. The cases ranged in severity from one where a lone pirate boarded a freighter, the *Ablasgracht,* while it was anchored off Cal Lao, Peru, and stole some rope, to another where crewmen on the reefer *Kamillo Sjenfuegoss,* while it was anchored off Guyana, turned away fifteen pirates in three boats by turning high-pressure fire hoses on them.[17]

Personal violence was involved, too, during that year. In May, seven armed pirates boarded the bulk carrier *Greece* in harbor at Rio Grande, Brazil. They injured two crew members with rifle butts and stole cash and valuables worth fifteen thousand dollars.[18] On the same day, five pirates boarded the containership *San Marino* at Rio de Janeiro. These criminals threatened to kill the crew and broke the seals on twenty-two containers. However, they took the contents of only two of them. This ship was also hit a second time by a force of ten armed pirates, again at Rio de Janeiro. The pirates used three boats to attack the ship after dark. Several crew members were held hostage while the ship was searched for money and valuables, and the pirates opened containers that were stowed aboard. A number of containers were opened and computer equipment stolen from them.[19]

In July, the bulk carrier *Kapitan Betkher* at anchor in the Port of Aratu, Brazil, was boarded by six pirates who took hostages and then beat and stabbed the ship's master. They then destroyed property and stole twenty thousand dollars from the master and crew.[20] In late April, pirates stole approximately eighteen thousand dollars in cash and valuables from a tanker at Santos, Brazil. The thieves held the crew at gunpoint and threatened to blow up the ship.[21]

Other incidents of piracy, involving varying degrees of severity, took place in the waters of Jamaica, Uruguay, Colombia, the Dominican Republic, and Ecuador.[22]

It should be noted that while 1996 was a violent year, it was not the first. Piracy around the world has been increasing almost on an annual basis, as noted in chapters 1 and 2, and the dangers it has posed have never been minimal. Between April and August 1994, there were seven attacks by armed pirates in the waters off Brazil. In several of those cases, hostages were taken, selected containers were forced open, and both cargo and the personal property of the crew were stolen.[23]

According to *Piracy and Armed Robbery against Ships,* published by the IMB and covering the period from 1 January through 31 December 1997, there were thirty-four reported incidents that occurred in the Americas to include ports in Ecuador, Jamaica, Venezuela, the Dominican Republic, Brazil, and the United States.[24]

Pirate attacks were of varying types and severity and involved numerous types of vessels to include tankers, containerships, reefers, and a ferry. Pirates, in several cases, were foiled in their attempts to board ships because of alert crew members, or escaped when they were discovered. In numerous other incidents, however, there was considerable theft and the level of pirate violence increased.

On 22 January, a ferry, *Rio Amazonia,* under way on the Amazon River in Peru, was attacked by armed pirates who then terrorized the crew and stole personal valuables, fuel, food, the ferry's radio, and approximately twenty thousand dollars in cash.[25]

The only incident occurring in the United States took place on 13 July when the general cargo freighter *Vanderpool Express,* while docked in Miami, was boarded by armed pirates who shot and killed the master and five crew members.[26]

On 4 June, the *Nordfarer* was boarded at Rio Haina in the Dominican Republic. Four pirates swam to the boat from the shore and boarded it armed with knives fastened to the ends of bamboo poles. They threatened to kill the watchman and the second officer while proceeding to loot the ship.[27]

BRAZIL—A SPECIAL PROBLEM

Brazil is the capital of piracy in the Americas and has been for several years. Indeed, according to the most recent available statistics, Brazil has become second in terms of piracy incidents and dangers in the world. The dubious honor of being first is still held by the waters off Indonesia and Thailand.[28]

The most serious piracy incidents reported by the IMB that occurred in Brazil during 1997 took place in March, May, and June. The first, on 9 March, involved the cargo ship *Libra Buenos Aires,* which was at anchor in the outer roads of Rio de Janeiro harbor. At about midnight, the ship was boarded by ten armed pirates who arrived alongside in speedboats and used grappling hooks to get on deck. The pirates threatened to kill the crew and then beat the master until he opened the ship's safe. After that the pirates searched all of the cabins for valuables and looted the containers. Although the pilot station in the harbor was notified and help was requested, no aid was provided by authorities.[29]

The next major pirate victim in terms of ship and crew was the *Ilya Ehrenburg,* a tanker berthed at the Alamoa Terminal in Santos, on 18 May. In this case six armed pirates gained access to the ship directly from the terminal and from the sea and began shooting. When some members of the crew who had not been seized by the intruders fired emergency rockets, the pirates left the ship. Police, contacted by radio, finally arrived almost an hour after being notified.[30]

Finally, five pirates attacked the crew of the *Al Burgan,* also berthed at the Alamoa Terminal in Santos, on 15 June. They walked onto the ship via an unguarded gangway. Cash in excess of ten thousand dollars was taken by the pirates; several of the crew members and officers were threatened at gunpoint.[31]

Each of these cases illustrates the serious problems that exist in Brazil's ports and that many observers link to an endemic laxness in security. However, other possibilities include government corruption, organized-crime influence, and related to both, the country's focal position in drug trafficking.

As a direct result of the problems experienced by shipowners over a number of years and related pressure being applied by several nations, the Brazilian government finally acted. In 1995, by presidential decree, the National Commission for Public Security in the Ports, Terminals, and Waterways was created. In addition, the presidential decree required the creation of state-level commissions that were to mirror the national one. The idea was to have an integrated program at both the state and national levels aimed at increasing security and reducing crime, including piracy. The effort was supported by the Baltic and International Maritime Council (BIMCO), which is offering detailed information on piracy attacks to the Brazilian police and port security officials to assist in relevant criminal investigations.[32] The International Maritime Organization (IMO), a part of the United Nations, has been offering information on piracy to Brazilian authorities since August 1995.[33]

Despite the ambitious aims and the presumably high level of government commitment, the situation in Brazil at least through the end of 1997 had not seen any noticeable improvements, as the IMB records illustrate. The earlier-mentioned cases involving the *Libra Buenos Aires, Ilya Ehrenburg,* and *Al*

Burgan are examples of what can and does happen all too frequently in Brazil's harbors, anchorages, and terminal facilities. In the *Libra Buenos Aires* case, assistance was requested but was not received. When the *Ilya Ehrenburg* called the police, they arrived some forty minutes later. And, of course, the attack on the *Al Burgan* was mightily aided by the fact that, for reasons apparently unknown, no watchmen from the terminal, although requested to provide some level of ship security, showed up until the attackers had left.[34]

Some, including the IMB in its 1997 report, tend to exhibit a certain kindliness in assessing the deplorable situation at the Brazilian anchorages and docks by citing lack of a coast guard and an insufficient amount of personnel and equipment to effectively battle piracy.[35] There are others who believe that there is more to the problem than a lack of resources. Indeed, having been generally accorded the status of being a major regional and economic power, Brazil's lack of ability, except in some exceptional cases, to deal with its mammoth problem of port security, remains a severe test of credibility.[36]

DRUGS, CRIME, AND CORRUPTION

Brazil has been named by the International Police Organization (Interpol) as being the third most favored place in the world for organized crime activity, the first two being Italy and the United States.[37] *Cosa Nostra, Camorra, 'Ndrangheta,* and *Sacra Corona Unita,* all organized-crime factions in Italy, are also operating throughout South America.[38] Brazil has been identified as a major trans-shipment point for cocaine produced in Bolivia and Colombia for export to the United States and Europe.[39]

While it is true that Brazil is not the only country in Central and South America that has drug and organized-crime groups operating within its boundaries, the nation's maritime system has been the most severely troubled and drugs may be a significant contributing factor.

Government corruption in Brazil was finally recognized in 1995. Port abuses, which included forcing shippers to pay bribes to expedite the unloading of cargoes and to avoid cargo loss and disappearance, began to be investigated by the Ministry of Justice.[40] According to shipper complaints, payoffs were allegedly made to customs officers, port administration personnel, and others.[41]

It does not require even a minimal level of expertise in criminal behavior and history to understand connections between government corruption and crime. But it never hurts to hear from authoritative sources. As noted in the U.S. Department of Transportation's *Maritime Security Report,* issued in January 1996:

> At the 1995 World Ministerial Conference on Organized Transnational Crime, the United Nations Economic and Social Council Report issued guidelines admonishing that corruption greatly facilitates the activities of organized criminal groups. The perception of official corruption emboldens organized crime groups to infiltrate or otherwise exploit legitimate businesses. Actual complicity on the part of port workers or longshore labor, could be of instrumental value to an organized gang engaged in such crimes as piracy and cargo theft.[42]

The unquestioned bottom line is that wherever one finds drugs and organized crime, there will be an environment in which crime will flourish, from the most petty to the most violent.

When pirates steal rope and paint, items that seem to have a particular appeal, these articles are obviously taken for disposal either through a fence or directly to a supplier of paint and rope who knows or should know the source of the merchandise. The money obtained from stolen property, whether that be such pedestrian items as rope or tools or more valuable things such as television sets and VCRs, can be used to buy drugs. The same is true when cash is stolen. It is probably not too much of a stretch to assume that cash obtained by pirates through theft is not used for the purpose of making commercial investments. Of course, in those incidents where pirates steal a quantity of valuable items such as TV sets, VCRs, computers, or other electronic equipment, the best sources to help dispose of such sophisticated merchandise are real fences. These are people who are almost always in league with, if not members themselves, of organized crime. The historical continuum between the merchant fences of the Golden Age and modern times is an interesting one.

Given a combination of laziness, inefficiency, and corruption in port areas, pirates seeking whatever kind of reward for their activities must surely feel a reasonably high degree of safety and security in their chosen means of commercial endeavor.

It is equally sure that when watchmen conveniently fail to appear at their posts until after pirates attack and leave, when the police fail to respond promptly when called, and when pirates can board a containership and proceed to open only those boxes where the most valuable cargo has been stored, that there is not only piracy afoot. Indeed, pervasive criminal activity exists that runs from the bustling docks of Rio de Janeiro, the anchorages of Santos, and the Alamoa Terminal, and high into the structure of law enforcement, the labor unions, and elsewhere.

Piracy, in Brazil now, as it was in the Golden Age, is a crime that exists where circumstances encourage it on the shore, as well as on the water.

Pirates at Work
Africa and Southeast Asia

The pirates and assorted other criminals who inhabit the maritime world have made the waters off both coasts of Africa, along with those of Southeast Asia, the most dangerous on earth. In terms of pirate attacks directed at commercial shipping, piracy emerged as a major problem beginning in the early 1980s, first off West Africa and then gradually spreading into Southeast Asia.[1]

Pirates in these locations murder, rob, and rape. Their particular selection of criminal behavior is generally dependent on the opportunities presented. And their skills are well honed. Most pirates in these waters come from fishing families that have made their living on the water for generations.

But there is much more.

Some pirates, wearing uniforms and using modern patrol craft, attack ships and sometimes actually hijack them. And along with this sort of charming event there are "phantom ships" (about which more will be said), maritime scams, rebels, and terrorists. Both of the latter groups carry out what are considered to be pirate activities, at least when the modern definition of "pirate" is used.

And, as mentioned in previous chapters, as bad as things have been over the past several years, they are getting decidedly worse both in terms of numbers of incidents and accompanying violence.

Having prepared the scene and the reader, we will now proceed to begin a tour of these infested waters with our starting point on the west coast of Africa. Our path will take us down the coast and up the eastern side of the continent and then into the Red Sea, the Indian Ocean, and beyond into the piracy hotbeds of the South China Sea, and the waters off the Philippines, Thailand, and Indonesia.

It should be noted that there are strong connections between conditions on land in Africa and what is happening on the water. In most of the African countries encountered, including Guinea, Sierra Leone, Ivory Coast, Ghana, Nigeria, Cameroon, Angola, Madagascar, Tanzania, Somalia, and Yemen, economic conditions are grim, government is corrupt, and political stability is nonexistent.

Piracy is new to this region. In recent years, the waters off Africa have been the scene of some of the most violent acts on record. One containership, the *Nedlloyd Steenkirk*, was attacked and boarded by pirates off Nigeria on 22 August 1982 and four crew members were wounded. A few days later, in port at Cotonou, Benin, another group of pirates boarded and stole cargo. At Lome, Togo, more cargo was stolen and while riding at anchor off Dakar, Senegal, the ship was again the victim of pirates. It proceeded to Banjul, Gambia, and was again boarded and robbed. Pirates again struck at Freetown, Sierra Leone, this time helped by the local police. The ship left port, leaving its cargo on the dock. During its final port of call at Monrovia, Liberia, additional cargo was stolen while the ship was berthed.[2]

Since that time, while no ship has experienced the same level of piracy, other cargo vessels have been victims of multiple attacks on the same passage.

Tankers, which usually (but not always) are targets of pirate interest principally because of crew member valuables, the contents of the ship's safe, tools, rope, and other sundry items, have been hit by pirates on a consistent basis off the African coasts. More meticulous records have been kept since 1986, which reflect this pattern.

AFRICA
Senegal

For many years Senegal has suffered from a dependence on low-yield agriculture, sporadic conflict with Mauritania over disputed territory, internal discord, and a virtually total alienation between the government and the people.[3] It has also been the scene of numerous pirate incidents during 1996 and 1997—the two years used here for general examination.

On 3 September 1996, while in the port of Dakar, a group of pirates came off second best to the crew of the tanker *Liberia,* which successfully used fire hoses against the marauders who were armed with machetes and steel sticks. Unfortunately, the pirates were wearing life jackets. During 1996 and 1997, there were several incidents of piracy in this harbor where armed pirates either successfully stole such things as rope and tools or were detected and fled.[4] In one case, on 27 September 1997, the crew of the American dredger *Northerly-Island* fired a shotgun at pirates, which had the desired end result of causing them to flee.[5]

Guinea

The economic situation and generally nonfunctioning government in Guinea has created a fertile breeding ground for crime both on land and on the water.[6]

On 27 March 1996, in the harbor at Conakry, the bulk carrier *Esperanza* was boarded by pirates from a speedboat. The thieves stole $3,150 from the safe and the effects of the crew.[7] In the same port, on 2 April 1997, at least twenty pirates, in a canoe but armed with automatic weapons, opened fire on the crew of the freighter *South County*. The ship heaved anchor and put to sea, escaping the pirates.[8]

Sierra Leone

Proceeding down the African coast, the next country with a good share of pirate activity in recent years is Sierra Leone. This nation is another that has been the scene of corruption, economic misery, overall political instability, and a war with Nigeria.[9]

In 1996, two particularly violent pirate attacks occurred. The first, on 12 October, involved a fishing boat the *Aley III*, which was boarded by hooded pirates who were armed with automatic weapons. Several crew members were injured and all were robbed.[10] On 8 December, the containership *Altair*, while in Freetown harbor, was boarded by fifteen pirates, all armed with submachine guns. The crew members were threatened, beaten, and robbed. Some containers were opened and cargo was stolen. The pirates left the *Altair* on a small boat, firing their weapons in the air as they departed.[11]

In 1997, the principal incidents of maritime violence in the waters of and around Sierra Leone were military ones, the result of Nigeria's attempts to enforce its embargo against its neighbor. On 11 September, the Kissey Fuel Jetty and the oil barge *Napetco I* were bombed by Nigerian aircraft and two barge workers were killed.[12] In August, Nigerian soldiers fired on the freighter *Seaway* and on the bulk carrier *Proteus*. There were no injuries suffered in either of the attacks.[13] Both incidents occurred in Freetown.

During 1996 and 1997, the ports of Abidjan, Ivory Coast, and Tema, Ghana, were the scenes of minor pirate thefts and attempted ones. On 6 January 1997, the bulk carrier *Jahan,* after having been reported sunk, was found at Tema under a new name. This incident, involving so-called phantom ships and other maritime frauds, will be discussed in a later chapter.

One other, far less glamorous, incident of piracy took place at Abidjan on 23 July where sixteen armed thugs boarded the tanker *Kimolos,* but were content to steal some rope.[14]

Nigeria

Nigeria, another severely troubled nation, both economically and politically, has been the scene of substantial piracy activity over the years. After a relatively quiet period during 1996 when only four incidents occurred, 1997 saw several major maritime attacks, one of which took place on 11 March and involved a group of tribesmen who took ninety oil rig workers hostage.[15] On 19 April in the harbor at Forcados, armed pirates boarded an unidentified ship and kidnapped the master.[16]

Another harbor incident, this one at Warri, occurred on 27 August. In that case several armed pirates boarded the freighter *Rugen* and robbed the master and crew.[17] About a month later, on 29 September, seven armed pirates boarded the freighter *Fischland* under way in a channel off Warri. The thieves robbed the crew and then ordered the master to open the ship's safe. The bridge was unmanned during the robbery.[18]

Nigeria's pirate troubles continued on 8 November when the freighter *Nadia J,* under way and leaving Warri harbor through a one-hundred-meter-wide channel and with a pilot on board, was seized by pirates with machine guns who threatened to kill the personnel on the ship's bridge. All of those on the bridge left it while the pirates stole rope and tools. It was through sheer luck that the ship did not run aground or collide with another vessel.[19]

Cameroon, Angola, and Madagascar

The harbors at Douala, Cameroon, and Luana, Angola, were the scenes of several piracy incidents during 1997. However, the cases were relatively minor and involved the theft of rope and other sundry items.

It is of historic interest to note the incidents of maritime crime occurring off the coast of Madagascar, which during the Golden Age was a haven for pirates. As a nation, Madagascar is the epitome of disaster with general strikes and revolutionary movements being the principal activities of the populace. The constitution, which was never taken too seriously, was rescinded in the early 1990s, and the nation's external public debt was rescheduled to prevent default.[20]

While 1997 witnessed only one maritime crime, this in Madagascar's harbor at Tomascino and involving petty theft, the Mozambique Channel, which separates the country from the east coast of Africa, is pirate infested. This is particularly true as that waterway opens into the Indian Ocean opposite Tanzania, Somalia, and Yemen.

Tanzania

Tanzania's experiences as a nation have been generally and consistently unpleasant, including intermittent warfare with the island of Zanzibar, which is actually part of its territory. In terms of piracy incidents, 1996 was a quiet time with only two reported incidents, both occurring in the outer anchorage of Dar Es Salaam. In one case, on 2 August, four pirates climbed the anchor chain of the tanker *Mimosa* and stole mooring ropes. They fled in a speedboat after being seen by the crew. Local authorities offered no assistance.

In 1997, reported incidents were notable because of the sheer number of pirates taking part in minor thefts. On 18 February, fifteen pirates boarded the container vessel *La Bourdannais,* attacked a watchman, and stole his walkie-talkie. On 17 June, at Dar Es Salaam, thirty-five pirates armed with rifles stole rope. On 23 August, the containership *Rejane Delmas,* while in harbor at Dar Es Salaam, was boarded by twenty-five armed marauders who apparently left the vessel without stealing anything.[21]

Somalia

Ships entering the harbors and transiting the waters off Somalia have experienced particularly high levels of trouble from pirates, some of whom are, or pose as, members of that nation's coast guard. Somalia is a special case when compared to virtually any other country in the world.

On 20 May 1996, a tugboat, while in international waters, was attacked by members of the Somali military who arrived in patrol boats and were armed with automatic rifles. The master and first officer of the tug were taken hostage and ten thousand dollars in cash and supplies were stolen. Some months later, on 25 September, the bulk carrier *Finnsnes,* while in harbor at Abidjan, was boarded by armed pirates who stole rope, paint, and similar items. The reefer *Scoff,* while in Somalian waters on 5 November, was fired on by pirates.

In 1997, things did not improve in the waters in and near Somalia. On New Year's Day, pirates attacked a Russian trawler and murdered its captain. The next day, pirates who identified themselves as members of the Somali Coast Guard, boarded the freighter *Clove* on the high seas. They demanded money that was, presumably, in exchange for not committing robbery or murder. The tanker *Helena,* on 7 March while off Somalia, had to increase speed to outrun two fishing boats that were firing at it with grenade launchers.

The next victim of pirates, on 17 April off Garad, Somalia, was a fishing boat, the *Bahari Hindi.* Armed pirates, believed to be members of one of the many Somalian warlord groups, shot a deck officer in the stomach and then hijacked the boat. The pirates demanded a $200,000 ransom, which was paid by the owners of the vessel.

Yemen

Yemen, the next nation on the way up the east coast of Africa, and another with significant and continuing internal problems, also has pirates operating off its shores.

On 25 April 1996, a yacht, the *SupFish 3,* was boarded in midafternoon while sailing off Yemen's shores. One of the people on the vessel was kidnapped.

GULF OF ADEN AND THE RED SEA

On 5 March 1997, a fishing boat sailing through these waters was hijacked by the crew who then took it to Bangkok, Thailand. On 5 April pirates in three small boats were reported to have opened fire on the tanker *Vasilius II,* within the Abu Ali Channel. The ship was able to escape.

Finally, near the Red Sea island of Zubair on 8 November 1997, pirates fired on the yacht *Poloflat.* They were repulsed in their boarding attempts by the yacht's owner who threw Molotov cocktails at them.

THE ARABIAN SEA AND INDIAN OCEAN

Over the years, these waters have been the scene of increasing, and more violent, incidents of piracy, a substantial number of them being the product of both terrorist and rebel activity.

In 1996, according to the IMB, pirate attacks in this area totaled twenty-six. Broken down more specifically, the numbers were two in Iran, eleven in India, nine in Sri Lanka, and four in Bangladesh.

The incidents that occurred during 1997 were greater, measured both by number (thirty-four) and by violence.

IRAN

The reported maritime crimes perpetrated in Iranian waters, and specifically, at the port of Bandar Imam Khomeini, totaled three. All of these occurred on 8 September and involved members of the Iranian revolutionary guards who detained two foreign registry tugboats and a barge.

INDIA

Pirates operating in these territorial waters boarded or attempted to board a number of ships during 1997. In a few cases the thieves were armed, but the thefts were minor: a television set was taken in one incident and rope was stolen in others. The crimes took place in the ports of Madras, Cochin, Tuticorin, and Kandla.

SRI LANKA

The incidents occurring during 1997 in and around Sri Lanka were numerous and violent. On 8 January at the Colombo anchorage, thieves boarded the cargo ship and opened several containers before fleeing. An unidentified vessel was seized on 12 February by soldiers in the belief that it was carrying Tamil rebels. According to the ship's master, the vessel was also attacked by government helicopters in territorial waters. The bulk carrier *Athena,* while anchored at Trincomalee on 29 May, was damaged by an explosion that may have been a bomb.

On 1 July, pirates reportedly attacked the freighter *Taraki* off Mannar. They fled when a naval patrol craft appeared. A few days later, on 11 July, the containership *Bunga Mas Lima,* while anchored at Colombo, was boarded by some thieves but, apparently, nothing was stolen.

The month of July also included far more serious incidents. In the first of these, the ferry *Missen* was set on fire by pirates, identified as Tamil rebels. Seven of the nine-member Indonesian crew were reported missing and are presumed dead. The other two crew members were released. In the second incident, the North Korean general cargo ship *Morang Bong* was hijacked by Tamil terrorists about five miles off Point Pedro where it had been anchored. The rebels claimed credit for the attack and announced that one crew member, the ship's fourth officer, Shing Gong Ho, had been killed. A coroner's report revealed that he had been shot through the head at point-blank range. The rebels moved the ship to Northern Jaffna and held it until 12 July where it and the crew were released to the International Committee of the Red Cross.

In September, four incidents of piracy took place. In one, on 5 September, the containership *CMV Fresena* was boarded at anchor in Colombo and the pirates fled as they were attempting to open containers. The same kind of pirate attacks occurred, also in Colombo harbor, on 21 September and 25 September. In the former case, the containership *Nuova Lloydiana* was boarded, containers were opened, and some color television sets were stolen. A similar attack occurred on 10 September at Colombo where the containership *Rajah Brooke* was boarded and nine containers were opened.

The bulk carrier *Cordiality,* while anchored off northeastern Sri Lanka on 9 September, had a far different experience. In that case, Tamil rebels using machine guns and rocket-propelled grenades attacked the ship. The Sri Lankan navy responded and engaged the rebels with the result that four crew members of the *Cordiality* were killed, and one is missing and presumed dead.

The IMB has noted that many of the coastline villages of Sri Lanka are populated by residents who have been pirates for generations. Their connections to the rebels, who have been engaged in a protracted civil war with the government, may be as much if not more born of mutual convenience than of political affinity.

BANGLADESH

The reported incidents that occurred during 1997 in Bangladesh were relatively minor. On 22 April and during May, at Mongla harbor, two freighters, the *Gold Spring* and the *Alam Talang,* were boarded or approached by pirates who, in the latter instance, stole rope. During July, four incidents took place, all of them at Chittagong. On 9 July, the bulk carrier *Bunga Kantan* was boarded and the pirates fled when observed. On 20 July, the tanker *Eburna* was boarded but with the same result. Finally, on 26 July, there were minor incidents involving the reefer *North Sea* and the tanker *Normar Splendour.* Months later, on 1 December, the tanker *Champion Trader,* again while at anchor in Chittagong, was boarded by two pirates who were seen and quickly fled.

SOUTHEAST ASIA

Southeast Asia, the most pirate-ridden place in the world by anyone's measure, is keeping a tight hold on that dubious honor. And in that region, Indonesia is up there with the leaders.

INDONESIA

During 1997, there were forty-seven maritime crime incidents in and around Indonesia compared with fifty-seven during the previous year. Most of these criminal acts took place in port or among the literally thousands of small islands that make up Indonesia's territory. The need for merchant ships to proceed slowly in the narrow channels that separate these islands makes the vessels attractive pirate targets.

Representative cases include those involving the tug *Maersk Bovavista* while at anchor in Balikpapan harbor on 20 January. Pirates boarded the tug without being seen and stole paint and tools. There were numerous such incidents throughout the year at Jakarta, Surabaya, Balikpapan, and Cigading. In addition, ships were attacked while under way, both within Indonesia's territorial waters and off the shores of that country.

Despite the fact that most of the piracy cases reported were of a minor variety, some of the incidents do stand out from the forty-seven acts of maritime crime perpetrated during 1997.

On 25 February, the bulk carrier *Siskin Arrow,* while alongside a dock, was boarded via the gangway by pirates who stole engine parts from the ship's store. They escaped on motorcycles. The ship's officers were advised not to report the incident because the police would detain the vessel. The tanker *Atlanta 95* was seized on 18 November while under way in the Arafura Sea. The pirates forced the crew to sail the ship to the Gulf of Thailand where the cargo of fuel was transferred to another tanker. Despite the removal of equipment from the ship, crew members were able to sail it to Singapore after they and the vessel were released by the pirates on 7 December.

The tanker *Petrobulk Racer* was the victim of pirates twice in one month. On 4 January, five pirates boarded it but quickly fled when the alarm was sounded. On 13 January, five pirates (possibly the same ones) boarded the tanker and again left when the alarm sounded. Both of these attacks occurred at Jakarta.

On 30 August, the same ship, while anchored outside the harbor at Jakarta, noticed a small boat off the tanker's bow. While this boat kept the attention of the crew, pirates from other small boats boarded the ship. One of the pirates held a knife to the third engineer's neck as other robbers boarded the ship. When they were finally observed, and the alarm was sounded, all of the pirates jumped overboard.

Earlier, on 30 May, while under way in territorial waters, the third officer of the cargo ship *Sinfa* was found shot, and the captain murdered. This is presumed to be the result of a pirate attack. The case remains under investigation.

THAILAND

While, again, there were numerous minor piracy acts that occurred around Thailand, most involved attempts to board that were unsuccessful or, if successful, resulted in the theft of such items as rope and paint. But the pirates here do seem more aggressive or less intelligent. On several occasions when ships' alarms were sounded, the pirates continued their crime. One example of this occurred on 20 August aboard the bulk carrier *Aro* in the harbor at Laem Chabang. Pirates stole numerous gallons of paint and were in no hurry to leave the ship when the alarm sounded. In another case, on 10 August, pirates boarded the containership *Oriental Bright,* despite the fact that flashlights were being trained on them. Once aboard, the pirates stole a variety of ship's stores. Earlier in the year, on 15 March, the ship had the interesting experience of being boarded while at anchor at Laem Chabang by a group of fifteen young girls and five men. In a fit of rage at being ordered off the ship, one of the girls told the master that the vessel would be robbed that night. Knowing that such an arrival was often used as a means of diverting the attention of the crew, the master put the ship on alert. The decision paid off when pirates, who tried to board the vessel several hours later by climbing the anchor chain, were repulsed.

There were several maritime incidents during 1997 that occurred in and around Cambodia, Myanmar, Malaysia, and Singapore.

CAMBODIA

According to the IMB, at least four ships were caught in the cross fire between rival groups of the Cambodian Navy that year. In the one reported piracy case, the tanker *Lung Shun 8,* while sailing off Cambodia on 5 February, was stopped by several fishing boats armed with machine guns and ordered to proceed to Ko Rong Island. Subsequently, the ship was forced to sail to Ronde Island. Eventually, the ship was released but personal valuables were stolen from the crew, and equipment and cargo were removed from the vessel.

MALAYSIA

In Malaysia, the unmanned yacht *Zaidenha,* anchored at Langkawi, was hijacked on 7 February and later found in Thailand. Three other incidents involved unsuccessful pirate boardings of the cargo ships *Ibn Qutaibah* on 28 June, *Thor Alice* on 8 September, and *Chris-T* on 29 November, in the port of Kelang, off Lahad Datu Sabah, and at Sandakan, respectively.

MYANMAR

Myanmar's waters have been reported as calm both in 1996 and 1997. Only one incident was reported in 1996 and two the following year. The 1997 cases occurred on 14 November at Yangon where the crew of the general cargo ship *Brilliant Pescadores* successfully repelled pirates who were attempting to board. Earlier, on 1 May, pirates boarded a ferry, took all of the passengers hostage, and released them after receiving payment.

SINGAPORE

In Singapore, both in harbor and while under way, there were a number of piracy incidents but most consisted of unsuccessful attempts to board or boardings that were discovered. However, in one case, involving the bulk carrier *Prabhu Jivesh,* on 3 November, pirates boarded, entered the captain's cabin, and stole jewelry and other valuables while holding the officer's wife hostage.

PHILIPPINES

Pirates, classified as terrorists, rebels, or just plain thieves, are extremely active in the Philippines. According to the IMB, thirty-eight piracy incidents occurred there in 1996 and fifteen in 1997. A number of piracy attacks occurred in this nation's harbors and on its waterways. The most flagrant cases involved such incidents as that which occurred on 23 February off Sirawai. In that incident, the ferry *Fortune* was attacked by seven suspected Muslim guerrillas who were part of the Moro Islamic Liberation Front (MILF). The pirates hijacked the boat, robbed the seventy passengers aboard it, and killed three who attempted to resist. On 13 March, another group of armed pirates attacked the passenger boat *Rakam* while it was under way off the Basilan islands. The marauders fired on the vessel, killing two people and wounding a number of others.

MILF terrorists were also responsible for the 29 April attack on the general cargo ship *Miguel Lujan* while it was berthed at Isabela. The ship was machine gunned and five people were wounded, two seriously. On the same day and at the same location, the passenger ferry *Leonara* was similarly attacked. Again, several people were wounded.

Finally, on 18 October, the containership *Yi He,* while at the Manila breakwater, was attacked by four armed pirates who boarded the vessel, robbed the ship's crew members, and shot and killed the fourth engineer. Local authorities reportedly did not respond to the scene, a fact that, given the officer's death from massive bleeding, may have been a factor in that fatality.

Last, on 20 December, in an incident that will be noted in a subsequent chapter dealing with solutions to the piracy problem, terrorists attempted to board the passenger ship *Sky Princess* while it was under way in Manila Bay. The pirates fired a rocket flare at the liner but did no damage.

THE FAR EAST

This area includes the waters encompassing the routes from Hong Kong to Luzon and Hainan. During 1996 there were four piracy attacks in that area as compared to only one in 1997. On 18 January, the cargo ship *Paramushir,* on the open sea, increased its speed to successfully outrun pirates.

SOLOMON ISLANDS AND PAPUA NEW GUINEA

Piracy attacks during 1997 that occurred in the Solomon Islands and Papua New Guinea were limited to two incidents involving yachts. On 8 August, pirates near the Solomons attacked the *Paccini III.* The pirates stole a small boat. On 16 May, the *Got-Cha-Covered* was boarded by seven armed men who robbed the crew.

VIETNAM

There were four piracy incidents near Vietnam during 1997. The first, on 28 March, occurred about ten miles off the coast and involved the containership *Ratana Sopa,* which, while under way, was fired on by men in a fishing boat. In the second, also off the coast, on 3 April, the cargo ship *Zim*

Kaohsiung I was fired on by a fishing boat. The third and fourth incidents occurred on 7 July and 8 July and involved the freighter *Oscar Venture* and the bulk carrier *Argonaut.* The first ship was in Haiphong and the second was at Hongai. Both were boarded by pirates who stole paint and rope. Police officers aboard the *Argonaut* arrested the thieves.

CHINA

The Chinese anchorages were the sites of two pirate attacks during the year. The first at Xinggang, involved the bulk carrier *Silver Sky,* which on 1 May, was boarded by pirates who attacked and injured the chief engineer. The second occurred at Chang Jiang where a ship was boarded by armed pirates who stole mooring ropes. The incident took place on 23 May.

On 12 September 1997, a group of pirates boarded the containership *Buxcrown,* opened some containers that were on deck, and stole some cargo. The most serious incidents took place on 11 October and 28 November in the waters off Hong Kong. In the first of these cases, the containership *Vosa Carrier,* while en route to Haiphong, was detained by Chinese officials. In the second, the cargo ship *Asian Friendship,* also while under way off Hong Kong, was boarded by security officers who forced the ship to a port in China.

The *Vosa Carrier* case is of particular interest because Chinese authorities confiscated all of the cargo. The officers and crew were interrogated and beaten by police. The ship and the crew were finally released on 12 November, almost a month after being seized and then only after the shipowners paid a cash fine of one hundred thousand dollars to the Chinese police.

EAST CHINA SEA

On 22 November, the general cargo ship *Sea Pioneer,* while on international waters in the East China Sea, was fired upon by a naval patrol boat, presumed to be Chinese, after being ordered to stop. The ship continued on its way despite eight or nine rounds being fired at it.

SOUTH CHINA SEA

Six piracy incidents took place during 1997 in the South China Sea, four more than were recorded for 1996. On 27 September, the tanker *Product Queen* was boarded by pirates who stole over thirty thousand dollars from the ship's safe. During November, four attacks occurred. On 5 November, the chemical tanker *Rahah* was boarded. The crew members were beaten and cash, documents, passports, and such personal items as shampoo and soap were stolen along with fresh water and fuel.

On 12 November, the tanker *Petro Ranger* was attacked by pirates who were repulsed by the crew. The next day, pirates armed with M-16 rifles were more successful in their boarding of the tanker *Michal* and stole several tons of bunker oil. On 26 November, the tanker *Theresa* was boarded by ten to twenty pirates all armed with M-16s. The pirates assaulted the crew members and held them at gunpoint while stealing cash, bunker fuel, and fresh water. One officer was shot in the leg.

Finally, on 6 December, the general cargo ship *Anabas* was boarded in the South China Sea by armed and uniformed pirates who forced the ship's officers to sail the vessel to Guangdon, China, where it was detained.

ALL VESSELS ARE TARGETS

It is important to note that, despite the lack of hard statistics, piracy attacks are not limited to commercial ships. Throughout Southeast Asia and, particularly, in the waters off Thailand and Vietnam, pirates attack fishing boats on a consistent basis. Many of these vessels are family operated and so, when seized, the pirates have not only the catch or the ship itself in mind. In many cases, the females are raped, often several times, and then murdered.

PHANTOM SHIPS AND MARITIME SCAMS

Fishermen, turned pirates, are often tools used to perpetrate this relatively new criminal endeavor. The real players are Southeast Asian-based crime syndicates with the money, knowledge, and connections to get started in this kind of enterprise. The syndicates can hire pirates as "muscle" to steal a vessel or, as an alternative, old ships can be legitimately purchased.

Container and bulk carrier ships as well as tankers, after being purchased or stolen, are then fraudulently registered and used to transport cargo under a false manifest. The cargo, of course, never arrives at the intended destination. It is, instead, transferred to another ship and the vessel and the cargo are sold to another buyer.

If the syndicate operates through the purchase, as opposed to the theft, of a cargo ship, it begins by buying an old vessel for about one million dollars, registering it under a new name with a flag-of-convenience country for about five thousand dollars, and then establishing "dummy" offices as fronts for the project. Ship documents will be very professionally forged. Crew members will be hired and given fake passports that reportedly come, in most cases, from Jakarta, Indonesia, or Bangkok, Thailand.

The ship is now ready to accept cargo from a shipper. In most cases, the cargo will be that with a high value and one that can be easily moved on the market. Once the vessel leaves port with the cargo aboard, the ship's name is again changed and perhaps the vessel is repainted.

In Southeast Asia, the ship is often sailed to Beihai, a Chinese port in the Gulf of Tonkin, where the cargo is off-loaded and put on the black market.

The IMB estimates that phantom ship schemes result in losses of some two hundred million dollars annually. When other maritime frauds are considered, losses reach a billion dollars.[22]

If the decision is made to steal a ship instead of purchasing one, pirates are selected to handle that task.

Perhaps the thus-far best-known case of successful hijacking of a ship is that of the freighter *Anna Sierra*. On 13 September 1995, this ship was seized by thirty armed pirates while sailing in the Gulf of Thailand. The crew was set adrift with only a small amount of food and water. The ship's cargo of sugar was worth an estimated five million dollars and it had left the port of Koh Si Chang, Thailand, the previous day with its destination being Manila.

It never arrived in the Philippines. The crew was picked up by fishermen off Vietnam.

Meanwhile, the pirates repainted the ship and renamed it the *Artic [sic] Sea* and sailed it to Beihai. At that point, forged documents were given to the pirate master.

The IMB learned of the forged documents and advised the Chinese authorities who promptly seized the ship. The Chinese then demanded proof as to the rightful owner of the cargo of sugar aboard the ship.[23] As of this date, the ownership of the *Anna Sierra* and its cargo have not been established to the satisfaction of the Chinese government. The cargo may by now have been auctioned. The ship was detained for nonpayment of harbor charges and was finally beached.

And the fate of the pirates? Unlike some pirates caught and punished in the United Arab Emirates, these pirates are not hobbling around minus legs or arms. After a period of detention aboard the ship that they had stolen, they were moved to a hostel and then released.[24] Presumably, these men, whose passports identified them as "entrepreneurs," are alive and well and searching for new ships to hijack.

During 1996, another ship, the tanker *Suci,* was attacked by armed pirates who forced the captain to sail the vessel to Horsburgh Lighthouse near Singapore where more pirates came aboard.[25] During the next day, 20 November, while under way on the ocean, the second and fourth engineers were put into a lifeboat and set adrift. While under pirate command, the stack was painted a different color, the vessel's name was changed to *Glory II,* and the ship was sailed to mainland China.[26]

A third incident of hijacking, mentioned earlier among the reported cases of piracy off the African coast, involved the freighter *Jahan,* which radioed a Mayday on 25 December 1996 while off Cape Town, South Africa, and stated that it was being abandoned. A widespread search, conducted over several days in good weather with calm seas, failed to produce any sightings of life rafts or wreckage.[27]

On 3 January 1997, the ship, renamed the *Zalcosea II,* was found in Ghana. The captain and crew were arrested for trying to sell the cargo. As may be considered typical in modern ocean shipping, the *Jahan*'s ownership is Panamanian, its registry is in Belize, and it is managed by a shipping firm in Singapore. The captain was from Ghana and his crew included Indian, Burmese, and Bangladesh nationals.[28]

And, of course, as noted in the above-reported cases, there are times when pirates, operating out of a highly developed sense of criminally motivated entrepreneurship, simply hijack a vessel and seek a ransom for the safe return of the ship and, possibly, crew members.

As can be readily seen from all of the reported incidents from this area of the world, pirate attacks are different from those generally perpetrated in, for example, Brazil. Many of the assaults occur on open water, some in daylight. And even more lethal weaponry than automatic rifles is commonly employed from the coast of Africa to the waters off Hong Kong.

In terms of motivations, the pirates here, as everywhere, have varied desires. Some steal rope and paint and others take entire cargoes or the ships themselves.

Without doubt, the pirates who have chosen to populate the waters off the coasts of Africa and eastward into Southeast Asia, are aggressive, skilled, violent, and, in many cases, in league with shore-based organized crime. One of these attributes is enough to create a serious problem. Taken in any kind of a combination, the problem converts into a true menace of the highest order.

The Economic Cost

For all the glamour and romantic aura surrounding eye-patch-clad and wooden-legged swashbucklers of days gone by, marine piracy is, has been, and always will remain, at its heart, a business endeavor. While the occasional abduction or theft at sea can be traced to either nationalism or terrorism, the object of most piracy is the acquisition of money. Viewed in that way, the target of most pirate attacks is chosen more to optimize the chances for economic success than to make a statement or to strike a blow for any particular geopolitical cause.

Since it is primarily a business—even for those who board ships in harbor and engage in petty theft—piracy must be analyzed with due consideration given to the incumbent capital investments, profits, and transaction costs. As shown by the recent increase in attacks, the piracy business is experiencing boom times. While the options available for decreasing the profitability of the activity to the point of eradication are mostly left to other parts of this book, this chapter analyzes the impact that the illicit business of maritime piracy has had on legitimate commerce. Specifically, the reactions of three related commercial activities to the threat of modern piracy will be explored: merchants using ocean-going vessels to transport their goods, shipping companies, and marine insurance carriers.

Unfortunately, financial statistics quantifying the cost of piracy have never been either systematically collected or tabulated with the result that much of the quantitative analysis is conjectural. According to Eric Ellen, executive director of the International Maritime Bureau (IMB) of the International Chamber of Commerce in England, "there are no organizations compiling statistics," and "the impact of piracy on the insurer [has] never been quantified."[1] In a May 1997 article in *The WorldPaper Online,* Harold Pieris estimates that reported pirate attacks alone account for losses of $200 million.[2] (All monetary amounts shown are in U.S. dollars.) Ellen has estimated that the total worldwide loss attributable to piracy is as high as $250 million yearly.[3]

As will be shown, however, a more rigorous analysis of the limited data available indicates that these estimates are probably too high. More likely, the total annual economic loss due to pirate attacks is no greater than $80 million.

Even using the more liberal estimates of financial losses due to pirate attacks, it is clear that piracy represents a relatively small financial burden on the industries involved when viewed in comparison to the gross value of merchandise moved across the world's waterways. Considered by the impacted industries as more of a nuisance than a threat, piracy has flourished in the absence of systematic resistance from entities engaged in legitimate maritime commerce. In simple economic terms, it appears that the commerce industries have not engaged in a concerted effort to stop piracy because the cost of doing so exceeds the revenue currently lost to pirate attacks. Leaving the human element aside (as we must for this chapter), taking the measures necessary to reduce piracy below its current activity level makes bad *economic* sense.

THE SCOPE OF THE PIRACY PROBLEM

To understand the reluctance of the commerce industries to actively combat maritime piracy, the economic losses attributable to the problem must be considered in contrast to the total amount of goods being transported across the world's waterways. While reliable estimates of global economic commerce are unavailable, according to estimates provided by the U.S. Office of Trade and Economic Analysis for 1995, the sum of the value of imports and exports to and from the United States alone was over $1.3 trillion.[4] Using a conservative estimate that 80 percent of the value of U.S. foreign trade is moved by sea, over $1 trillion was shipped as ocean cargo between the United States and other countries in 1995.[5] Assuming, first, that American sea commerce constitutes no more than half of the world's seagoing cargo (by value) and, second, that intercoastal commerce among American ports is negligible (both very conservative assumptions), at least $2 trillion in commerce was at sea during 1995. Table 5.1 depicts the estimated maritime commerce for the years 1991 through 1996 using the above assumptions.

Although the figures on maritime piracy are enormous in the abstract they are dwarfed by the $2 trillion of commerce actually at sea in any given year. According to statistics compiled by the IMB's Regional Piracy Centre in Kuala Lumpur, 188 pirate attacks were reported in 1995. As noted in other sections of this book, however, "pirate attacks" is a very general term, used to describe several different crimes, each with different *modus operandi* and with very different financial consequences. Table 5.2 categorizes the types of pirate attacks reported worldwide for the seven years from 1991 through

Table 5.1. Minimum Estimates of World Maritime Commerce, 1991–1996

YEAR	MINIMUM ESTIMATE OF ANNUAL WORLD MARITIME COMMERCE (U.S. $)	UNITED STATES FOREIGN TRADE (U.S. $)
1991	908,800,000,000	1,454,080,000,000
1992	980,900,000,000	1,569,440,000,000
1993	1,045,750,400,000	1,673,200,640,000
1994	1,176,500,000,000	1,882,400,000,000
1995	1,328,187,000,000	2,125,099,200,000
1996	1,420,364,300,000	2,272,582,880,000

Source: U.S. Bureau of the Census, *Statistical Abstract,* 1991, 1992, 1994; *World Almanac and Book of Facts,* 1995, 1997, 1998.

1997 (inclusive). For the purposes of this chapter, it is useful to analyze "pirate attacks" within two distinct subgroups: hijackings, in which the intent is to steal the entire cargo and the ship, and "muggings" in which the intent is to steal the easily pilferable property of the ship and crew.

Capt. Jayant Abhyankar, deputy director of the IMB, in England, estimates that the average economic loss due to ship hijacking is between $1 and $2 million per attack, but that the average loss for other pirate attacks (which he terms "maritime muggings") is approximately $5,000.[6] It is important to note that many reported attacks result in no economic loss, since the incidents tabulated by the IMB include attempted (but unsuccessful) boardings and other inchoate acts of piracy. Applying Abhyankar's most liberal estimates to the data supplied in Table 5.2, the total economic loss from reported pirate attacks in 1995 was no greater than $24,880,000.

The data derived above must be corrected to account for the number of pirate attacks that remain unreported. Ellen was quoted in the *Christian Science Monitor* in 1992 as having estimated that no more than 1 percent of piracy incidents are reported.[7] Recently, however, he estimated that between 40 and 60 percent of pirate attacks are reported to the IMB or to the United Nations' International Maritime Organization and are then included in the IMB's annual analysis.[8] It is likely that almost all unreported incidents were muggings rather than hijackings, both because of the added visibility of ship hijackings and the fact that shipowners and merchants generally stand to recover much more from their insurers on reporting a hijacking than a mugging. As Captain Abhyankar has noted, the average mugging loss of $5,000 is "usually below the deductible level under the insurance cover."[9] Because of that fact, the insured stands to make no financial gain by reporting any loss below the policy deductible.

Even assuming that only 40 percent of all incidents are reported, the total estimated economic loss for all pirate attacks worldwide during 1995 was no greater than

Table 5.2. Comparison of the Types of Attacks Reported during the Years 1991–1997

CATEGORY	1997	1996	1995	1994	1993	1992	1991
Attempted boarding	14	36	27	22	33	18	4
Vessel boarded	163	175	127	49	28	80	101
Hijack	14	5	12	5	—	1	1
Robbery/Theft at port	2	5	2	5	8	—	—
Vessel fired upon	26	6	9	—	16	6	—
Detained	7	—	11	6	8	—	—
Others	3	1	—	3	10	1	1
TOTAL	229	228	188	90	103	106	107

Source: International Maritime Bureau, *Piracy and Armed Robbery against Ships,* March 1998.

$62,200,000. This should be considered a very liberal estimate since it hinges on the assumption that high-loss hijackings represent the same percentage of unreported pirate attacks as do unreported ones. To illustrate the power of this liberal assumption, if all hijackings were reported and only 40 percent of the muggings were reported, the total estimated economic loss for 1995 would be considerably less: $26,200,000.

Therefore, the most liberal estimate of economic loss for 1995 due to piracy is $62,200,000, as compared to a conservative one of total worldwide maritime commerce in that same year of over $2 trillion. In perspective, the economic cost of maritime piracy is essentially negligible, representing no more than .0029 percent of all shipped goods, or a mere 29.3 cents for every $10,000 shipped by sea. Table 5.3 recreates the calculations for the years 1991 through 1997 (inclusive), based on the same assumptions discussed above.

Table 5.3. Estimate of Economic Loss Due to Piracy during the Years 1991–1997

YEAR	REPORTED HIJACKINGS	OTHER REPORTED ATTACKS	TOTAL ECONOMIC LOSS (U.S. $)	PERCENTAGE OF ALL COMMERCE	CENTS LOST PER $10,000 SHIPPED
1991	1	106	6,325,000	.0004	4.3
1992	1	105	6,312,500	.0004	4.0
1993	0	103	1,287,500	.0001	0.8
1994	5	85	26,012,500	.0014	13.8
1995	12	176	62,200,000	.0029	29.3
1996	5	223	27,787,500	.0012	12.2
1997	14	215	72,687,500	.0032	32.0

Source: Jayant Abhyankar.

While the data in Table 5.3 indicate a general perceptible increase in the economic loss due to pirate attacks throughout the 1990s, the 1997 loss rate is still only 32.0 cents for each $10,000 shipped, a number too insignificant to attract much notice among the corporate bookkeepers. The general trend continued through the first half of 1998. For the first six months of that year, the IMB reported eighty-six pirate attacks, seven of which were hijackings.[10] Using the calculations that formed the basis for Table 5.3, these statistics project a total estimated worldwide economic loss for 1998 of $71,975,000, which equates to .0032 percent of the total goods shipped or 31.7 cents per $10,000 shipped—figures roughly equivalent to 1995 and 1997 ones.[11]

The rate and economic impact of pirate attacks are not constant worldwide, however, and regional differences may be important in analyzing the responses of those in maritime commerce to the threat posed by modern piracy. As discussed elsewhere in this book, differences in enforcement mechanisms, crew training, regional economic well-being, the types of vessels employed, and even tacit or explicit support from particular nations lead to wide variations in the frequency and nature of pirate attacks in different maritime regions around the globe. Simply put, the odds of navigating a maritime cargo safely from Boston to New York are far more favorable than transiting the same cargo through the Phillip Channel between Indonesia and Singapore.

Recognizing the regionality of the piracy threat, the IMB now reports its piracy data by region. Table 5.4 reflects the data provided by the IMB for the year 1997 and the estimated economic loss, tabulated by region.

Table 5.4 clearly depicts the regionality of piracy's economic impact. The Southeast Asian region, including Indonesia, Thailand, Malaysia, the Philippines, Cambodia, Myanmar, and Singapore, was the site of over one-third of

Table 5.4. Types of Attacks by Maritime Region, 1997

MARITIME REGION	HIJACKS	OTHER TYPES	ESTIMATED ECONOMIC LOSS
Southeast Asia	7	84	36,050,000
Far East	0	19	237,500
Indian subcontinent and Persian Gulf	2	32	10,400,000
Americas	0	34	425,000
Africa	3	38	15,475,000
Other locations	3	7	15,087,500
TOTAL	15	214	77,675,000

Source: International Maritime Bureau, *Piracy and Armed Robbery against Ships,* March and July 1998.

the reported pirate attacks in 1997. Pirates in Southeast Asian waters made off with almost half of the booty taken worldwide.[12]

Even within a given maritime region, it is clear that some areas are more dangerous than others. The waters in and around Indonesia saw forty-seven pirate attacks during 1997, with an estimated economic loss of approximately $5.6 million. The waters off Thailand, the Philippines, and Sri Lanka accounted for approximately $10.15 million each. Meanwhile, almost half of the attacks and economic loss reported in the Western Hemisphere occurred off the coast of Brazil. These five major trouble spots alone witnessed 106 pirate attacks with a total value of $36,237,500, which is roughly half of the worldwide total in each respect.

Although the figures provided by the IMB for the first six months of 1998 do not contain sufficient information to calculate the economic loss for each region, the raw numbers of pirate attacks reported in each area identify some of the same problem zones as do the 1997 statistics. Of eighty-six attacks reported through 30 June, eighteen (21 percent) occurred in and around Indonesia and thirteen (15 percent) near the Philippines.[13]

Even given the relatively high concentration of pirate activity in Southeast Asia, however, the economic losses there remain too small to significantly impact the merchants, shippers, and insurers doing maritime business in the region. As noted by the IMB in its March 1998 special report, *Piracy and Armed Robbery against Ships:*

> Therefore in statistical terms, the probability of a ship being boarded when passing through this area [the Phillip Channel] is relatively small and, as the consequence is limited to loss of money or money's worth, basic risk management comes into operation and the cost of prevention must not exceed the cost of the problem. There are security organizations offering all types of guarding and escort systems in the area, which, although possibly effective, would be completely uneconomic.[14]

Deterring piracy is, at best, an expensive proposition. According to the IMB, the Thai government, with United Nations support, set up an antipiracy unit in 1980. After eight years of operation, the unit had spent approximately $13 million and had not yet caught a single pirate.[15] While the possibility that the Thai unit deterred some acts of piracy in a relatively high-occurrence zone cannot be discounted, it should be noted that, compared to the economic loss rates due to piracy in Thailand and worldwide, a figure of $13 million dollars over eight years in a single region is a huge cost for a preventative measure of such questionable efficacy. In this case, the ounce of prevention may not be worth the pound of cure. As long as piracy remains at levels where the financial risk equates to approximately 31.7

cents on $10,000, businesses engaged in maritime commerce will have little incentive to take the steps necessary to eradicate, or even to seriously combat, the piracy problem.

The Shipping Industry's Response

Even though the economic balance between risk and prevention weighs so heavily to the side of risk that shippers are effectively discouraged from expending any resources to deter pirate attacks, the *human* cost has driven shippers to take some modest steps. From a purely economic point of view, of course, shippers have realized that there is some risk of pirate attack, most particularly in those trouble spots noted earlier, and they understand their own liability for cargoes lost in transit. As economically rational actors, shippers will attempt to deflect as much of the economic risk occasioned by pirate attacks as is possible and practical, and will pass on any increased cost to other parties.

Under the ancient laws of bailment, a shipper carrying a merchant's cargo has an absolute duty to deliver the cargo safely to the merchant or its designated recipient, and is generally liable for the loss of that cargo, whatever the cause, including pirate attack.[16] Unless the merchant and the shipper specifically agree to assign the risk of loss differently in the shipping contract, the shipper is responsible to the merchant for the loss.

In most cases, shipping companies transfer this risk back to the merchant by "contracting out" of their liability as bailees, an option specifically permitted by the common law of bailment.[17] When the shipper and the merchant include such an indemnity clause in the shipping contract, the shipper is then absolved of all liability to the merchant arising out of any loss of the cargo that might occur in transit.

In other cases, the shipping companies may decide to cover their risk by purchasing marine insurance, which specifies that the insurer will reimburse the shipper for its economic loss suffered due to casualties at sea, including, to be shown later in this chapter, incidents of piracy. As with all insurance, the large number of shippers purchasing such policies permits the insurers to spread the risk of loss due to piracy among the industry participants, which, in turn, minimizes the impact of the piracy threat on any individual shipper and tends to equalize the effect of piracy on all of the maritime carriers.

Finally, some shippers choose to self-insure, or to "go bare," a decision that exposes them and the merchants who utilize their services to financial ruin in the event of pirate attack or any other marine disaster. In the long run, these shippers are not likely to operate successful businesses, since they not only risk their own financial ruin in the event of a pirate attack on their vessels but also may subject their merchant customers to significant economic setback. Most merchants avoid using uninsured carriers (unless the carrier is sufficiently capitalized to adequately self-insure), opting instead for the greater financial security offered by a carrier backed by a solvent insurance company.

Even those shippers who properly and adequately insure their cargoes run the risk of some financial loss due to piracy. Liability insurance policies, including those covering cargo, almost always include a "deductible"—an amount that the insured agrees to pay before the insurer becomes responsible for any reimbursement. On the large-scale policies necessary to adequately cover oceangoing commerce, premiums are affordable only when the policyholder agrees to absorb a large deductible. Further, as discussed earlier, very few pirate attacks are of the "hijacking" type in which the entire cargo and ship are targeted. Almost always, pirate attacks are focused on the cash and property of the crew and the ship itself. Most often, the economic loss incurred as a result of these attacks is insufficient to exhaust the deductibles on the marine insurance policies, meaning that the entire loss must be borne by the shipper.[18] It should be noted, too, that this principle applies whether the merchant or the shipper is the insured.

Factors other than the pure economic loss resulting from pirate attack may lead a shipper to act in protection of its vessels and crews. First, the very violent nature of modern maritime piracy creates an atmosphere in which it is much more difficult for a shipper to crew its vessels, particularly those that frequent the shipping lanes in Southern Asia and around Brazil. As a consequence, the shipper must offer better pay and increased benefits to its sailors in compensation for their greater physical risk, driving up the shipper's operating expenses as a result. Indisposed to acting altruistically, the shipper then transfers this cost to the merchant in the form of higher cargo rates. Only when higher rates make the shipper less attractive to a merchant than competitors, will that shipper be inclined to adopt measures designed to minimize the piracy risks faced by its crews.

Second, shippers whose operations appear to be more susceptible to pirate attacks, or who have a reputation of being vulnerable, are less likely to attract well-paying merchant customers.[19] To remain in business, such shippers would need to cut prices and reduce margins to compensate merchants for their own added risk of delay or loss, a point that will be further explored in this chapter. In order to avoid having to reduce profit margins to stay in business, shippers are best advised to employ antipiracy strategies at least as advanced and sophisticated as those employed by the majority of their fellow shipping companies.

Several methods for reducing the risk of piracy are available to the shipper, varying widely in cost and efficacy. The method selected by a given shipper, if any, will depend on the perceived threat, the economic risk presented by the threat, and the economic pressure felt by the shipper to implement security measures. Possible actions range from arming the ship and its crew to training personnel in the use of high-pressure fire hoses to repel boarders.[20] Some shippers may elect to forgo certain pirate-infested waters entirely, resulting in even higher shipping rates to the troubled areas as the supply of ships willing to transit such zones decreases while the demand for such transport remains constant.

Implementing the more effective of these measures often costs more than shippers are currently willing to spend. As noted by E. Cameron Williams, "suggestions to train and arm seafarers, provide detachments of armed security personnel to ships transiting dangerous waters, or to provide nonlethal defensive systems to merchant ships have all been rejected as too expensive by owners."[21] Several recent pirate attacks reported by the IMB, however, reflect successful efforts by crew members to repel boarders by using the spray from pressurized fire hoses, indicating that some of the less costly measures and training are being used by at least some shippers.[22]

Recognizing the increased efficiency of pooling their resources to combat a peril suffered by all, the shippers have formed several international organizations designed to educate both governments and other shippers on the trends and tolls of modern piracy. Such organizations as the IMB's Regional Piracy Centre, the Baltic and International Maritime Council, the International Shipping Federation, the Singapore National Shipping Association, and the Safe Navigation Committee of the Asian Shipowners' Forum have each dedicated a significant portion of their resources and efforts to providing a united front to combat maritime piracy. These groups also serve as data collection repositories on the locations and methods of pirate attacks, and the booty targeted by pirates in different regions of the world.

The experience and expertise of these organizations is then offered to all shippers in response to the common threat of pirate attack. The Regional Piracy Centre in Kuala Lumpur, Malaysia, does extensive work in the investigation of, and data compilation on, pirate attacks and issues regular status reports on pirate activity over marine radio.[23] In its annual report, the IMB has included a chapter on practical shipboard procedures for use by shippers in helping to prevent acts of piracy.[24]

THE IMPACT ON MERCHANTS

Merchants themselves may be faced with the cost of losing the value of their cargo if the shipper does not fully insure it or if the shipper's insurer is insolvent. While the laws of bailment generally shift the liability for lost cargoes from the merchant to the shipper while at sea, shippers often obtain indemnification protection from merchants for lost goods through explicit provisions of the shipping contract.

Even absent such indemnification, some small shipping lines may carry cargoes with values in excess of the worth of the shipping company. In that case, of course, a shipper who falls victim to pirate attack simply would not have the funds available to fully reimburse the merchant, leaving the merchant to account for the remainder of the loss. This situation is most likely to occur when a shipper operates only a single vessel, since a hijacking of that ship would deplete the shipper of its sole asset of significant value.

Merchants often purchase insurance themselves to cover cargo being shipped. This practice, however, marginally increases the cost of shipping and may affect the competitiveness of the merchants' products in the marketplace. As an alternative, merchants may refuse to accept liability for cargo loss and may further require that the shippers used be either adequately insured or financially stable enough to reimburse for the loss of cargo in the event of pirate attack. The transaction cost of verifying such compliance is minimal, particularly if a merchant uses the same shipping line on a repetitive basis. Some merchants choose to avoid the investigation cost altogether by selecting shippers of greater renown—not necessarily the best or most cost-effective solution since even a famous or traditional name may mask a firm experiencing significant financial problems and because "big name" carriers may ultimately charge higher shipping rates.

In addition to the purely economic loss suffered by merchants when pirates steal their cargoes, there are very real long-term business consequences to earning a reputation as an unreliable supplier. Tonnage lost at sea to pirates means empty store shelves or unfilled orders at the scheduled destination. The cash value of the goods lost to pirates can usually be reimbursed through insurance or subsequent price increases, but losses to competitors because a merchant's products are not on the shelves or are not available to fill a rush order may not be so easy to recoup. In fact, according to Eric Ellen, one of the reasons that many pirate attacks remain unreported is that the resulting delays in delivering the goods creates a market disadvantage greater than the advantage gained (if any) by reporting anything but the most costly pirate incident.[25] The bureaucratic problems arising from filing a report of a piracy attack—at least in some parts of the world—are well known throughout the maritime industry.

More likely, in the short term, merchants will seek the services of shippers that have demonstrated an ability to make timely deliveries free from pirate attack. Such carriers, as already noted, will necessarily charge the merchants increased rates due to the cost of whatever antipirate measures they may undertake. We should, of course, expect merchants to pass along the increased cost of transport to the ultimate customer in the form of product price increases.

Certain merchants may find, however, that the market will not bear the necessary price increases, particularly if competitors in the marketplace are able to minimize their own antipiracy price hikes. In the most likely scenario, businesses operating out of high-occurrence piracy regions will be at a significant market disadvantage when compared to those sailing through waters that are pirate-free. Merchants who manufacture their products in Southeast Asia, for example, are likely to experience greater losses due to piracy than those who operate in North America because the former's goods must, of necessity, pass through high-risk piracy zones regardless of the ultimate destination.

The competitive marketplace will thus force these disadvantaged merchants to move their operations out of pirate-ravaged countries (such as Thailand, Sri Lanka, and the Philippines) and to relocate in nations that are relatively pirate-free in order to avoid losing customers to lower-priced competitors. While costly at the start, such relocation promises to be the best long-term solution for merchants in high-occurrence piracy zones if, and when, piracy begins to be more than a mere nuisance financially.

THE INSURERS

The basic purpose of any insurance scheme is to spread the risk of costly, but improbable, financial loss among many participants vulnerable to the risk. Each risk participant has an "expected loss" due to the risk, which is equal to the probability of an occurrence multiplied by the average loss sustained in an occurrence. For an insurance scheme to work, the insurer must collect, in premium payments, from the various participants, sufficient funds to reimburse the losses in accordance with the policy provisions while concurrently retaining a portion of the sum collected as its profit. Clearly, the insurer must charge premiums somewhat higher than each participant's projected loss in order to create a profit for itself.

Viewed collectively, insurance of any kind is a poor business proposition for the policyholders who, *collectively,* pay more to the insurer than they would have to lose on the risk. From the viewpoint of an individual insured, however, the security and stability provided by insurance against sudden financial ruin due to a single catastrophic occurrence will usually outweigh the gradual financial loss generated by repeated insurance premiums. Able to pass along the relatively small cost of insurance premiums to its ultimate consumer, the policyholder effectively "buys" commercial stability through insurance at the cost of the difference between the premium payment and its expected loss. In that way the insurance business flourishes, especially in contexts where the potential loss due to a particular risk is especially high and the probability of occurrence is especially low—the exact characteristics of the modern piracy threat.

Maritime commerce industry participants have recognized the value of insuring against loss at sea since the very early days of waterborne shipping. As early as 3000 B.C., Chinese merchants often spread their risk of loss by dividing their shipments among several vessels headed for the same destination so that the loss of any one vessel would not result in a devastating economic loss for any one merchant. No later than 916 B.C., merchants in Rhodes instituted a system of "general average," by which any loss at sea would be reimbursed by pro rata contributions by fellow merchants. By 1255 A.D., the merchant state of Venice had created a modern insurance scheme, collecting premiums from merchants in exchange for reimbursement in case of pirate attack, spoilage, or theft. In 1688, Lloyd's of London began underwriting marine insurance policies, and the maritime insurance industry has been "big business" ever since.

Insurers generally offer a number of different types of marine insurance policies, some of which specifically name the perils covered, while others cover all risks. In most cases, policies that specifically name the perils covered do not include losses due to piracy.[26] As a result, many shippers and merchants who obtain cargo insurance—and even some who *believe* they are covered for piracy loss—may have their claims for piracy losses rejected because the insurance contract they purchased did not cover the marine piracy risk.

As is the practice with other liability-type insurance policies, marine insurance contracts usually set both policy limits and deductibles. Policy limits cap the maximum amount an insurer may be required to pay to an insured for a given policy period and/or for a single loss. While the policy limits are often high, in some cases the loss sustained due to a ship hijacking may exceed the policy limit. In such a case, the policyholder would receive no reimbursement from the insurer for the excess and is left to its own devices to cover the remainder of the loss. Excess insurance, which can cover the policyholder for losses beyond the limits of the primary coverage, may be available from some insurers to help protect against the loss.

While policy limits set the *maximum* reimbursement to be paid by the marine insurer, deductibles establish the *minimum* value for which the insurance policy must respond. For each individual occurrence and/or for each policy period, the shipper or merchant is required to absorb all costs up to the deductible amount. The insurer is responsible only for losses sustained that exceed the amount of the deductible—a figure that is determined by negotiation between the insurer and the insured. A lower deductible amount generally means a higher premium as the insurer must be compensated for its added liability. Policyholders tend to find that *first dollar* policies—those with no deductibles—are too expensive and, as a result, most marine policies have some deductible amount. Because piracy losses are usually less than the policy deductible, insurers are required to indemnify such losses only on rare occasions.[27] Even when the shipper or merchant is adequately covered, the shipper will find itself financially responsible for almost all piracy losses unless, of course, a ship is hijacked.

Because they actually bear very little financial risk occasioned by piracy, insurers have done very little to quantify or diminish the losses caused by pirate attacks. Insurance companies normally collect and carefully scrutinize data on all possible risks in order to ensure that, in the aggregate, the sum of policy premiums will exceed the sum of payments due to covered losses. As noted by Matthew Marshall of the Institute of London Insurers, piracy is "only one of a number of risks accepted by insurers when they rate marine insurance business, and is not normally counted or quantified separately."[28] Although Marshall notes that insurers may charge a higher premium for goods destined to areas in which pirate attacks occur more frequently, he doubts that any insurer has conducted full actuarial studies of the risk and instead thinks that any increased premium would be "based on the insurer's shrewd understanding of the additional risk rather than any scientific calculation."[29]

If the piracy risk continues to increase as it has over the past decade, insurers will be forced to collect actuarial data on pirate attacks and to adjust their premiums accordingly. The first wave of actuarial data is likely to reflect a worldwide assessment of piracy and will probably lead to increased policy premiums for all shippers and merchants carrying piracy insurance, regardless of their destination.

As the actual data become more refined, however, insurers will seek to lower their premiums when possible to compete for less risky business, shifting the burden of funding piracy insurance onto those goods sailing through the most dangerous waters. Eric Ellen reports that, already, insurers have begun to charge increased premiums because of the piracy risk in some regions, and that it is more difficult to obtain hull insurance in Indonesia than elsewhere.[30] This inevitable response to an increased piracy threat will further aggravate the price differentials between goods bought and sold in areas of high pirate activity and those in safer regions. The economies of those countries in the trouble areas will, as a result, be weakened by increased consumer prices of imports and the loss of even more manufacturing jobs from the region. A corollary problem will conceivably be that of increased difficulties in attracting direct foreign investment.

THE ROLE OF GOVERNMENTS

Presently, the most significant and visible effect of piracy is its *human* toll, not its economic one. Because the economic cost, in relative terms is rather small, there is very little incentive for those economically impacted by the piracy problem to take the steps necessary to fight it. Governments, however, in their role as protectors of citizens as well as guardians of their respective economies, have a decided and recognizable interest in eradicating piracy as a threat in the waters surrounding their borders.

Governments, both individually and collectively, represent a greater number of persons affected by piracy than do the shippers, merchants, or insurers. Consequently, governments are best able to spread the costs of combating piracy and are able to mount the most cost-effective programs. Of the possible actors reviewed in this chapter, only governments may have a positive economic incentive to act to curb maritime piracy. Not all governments have the same resources to target the problem, however, and a review of the regional statistics on piracy set out earlier in this chapter indicates clearly that the poorest regions are also those most prone to pirate attacks.[31]

Despite their comparative inability to do so, governments in the poorer regions of the world have the most to gain by effectively ridding their seas of marine pirates. The weaker economies will more keenly feel the increased consumer prices and loss of manufacturing jobs that will surely follow a continuing rise in pirate activity. Such economic impact may very well lead to a downward spiral in which increased unemployment and regional poverty will serve to encourage more individuals to try their hand at the piracy business—thereby increasing the regional piracy risk and accelerating economic troubles. Clearly, the governments presently least able to control piracy are those with the most to lose.

But modern piracy represents a real threat not only to the poorer regions, but to the wealthier ones as well. For some time, experts have recognized the possibility of environmental catastrophe occasioned by pirate attack. As reported by *Fortune* in 1991:

> Piracy may someday exact a far higher cost—one not payable in dollars only. When a crew is busy repelling boarders and its captain is being handcuffed to the rail, who's minding the ship? Says Michael Gray, a writer for *Lloyd's List International,* a shipping newspaper: "I worry about one of these tankers or chemical carriers running aground because the captain has a gun to his head. It could be the most colossal environmental disaster."[32]

The IMB has, indeed, predicted that a grounding of a supertanker similar to the *Exxon Valdez* in the Phillip Channel between Singapore and Indonesia would cause oil pollution that "would extend well into the Malacca Strait, eastwards to beyond the Horsburgh Light and, given the necessary combination of wind and tide, the oil would completely surround Singapore Island and the multitude of islands which form this part of Indonesia."[33] While pirate-infested seas such as those in Southeast Asia would be the most likely ones to host the environmental disaster described above, it is abundantly clear that the entire maritime world is actually at risk. Lethal cargoes are transported everywhere and there are no borders that limit pirate activity. The problems and possibilities of environmental disaster and piracy are fully covered elsewhere in this book.

Whether the concern is viewed primarily as economic, human, or environmental, collective and individual action by governments represents the only likely solution to the global piracy problem. The other entities involved in maritime commerce simply do not have the proper economic incentives to wage an effective war on piracy. Without a cost-effective reason for doing so, shippers, merchants, and insurers cannot be expected to take the steps necessary to crush the pirate threat.

THE NEED FOR GOVERNMENT INTERVENTION

It can be statistically demonstrated that at present activity levels, maritime piracy has little effect on international commerce. Even with the large upturn in piracy attacks during the past five years and the steadily increasing number of ship hijackings, the overall impact of piracy adds a financial risk of less than forty cents on every ten thousand dollars shipped worldwide. In certain regions, particularly the Indian subcontinent and Southeast Asia, extraordinarily high levels of piratical activity increase the economic risk substantially. But even in those areas, the threat of piracy lies below the surface of financial visibility, essentially unseen by shippers, merchants, and insurers—all of whom maintain a steady gaze only at the bottom line.

Yet the undeniable and apparently continuing trend of increased pirate activity presents a concern for all in what may well be the near-term future. Left unchecked, piracy will begin to become visible and maritime commerce industry participants will react accordingly. Marine insurers will raise premiums on their protection and indemnity policies, shippers will charge increased rates to cover both the costs of implementing antipiracy measures and the higher wages of crews who will demand more money for hazardous duty. Merchants will respond to these increases by raising the prices to be paid by the ultimate consumer. Governments will be forced to intervene to protect their economies as well as their seafaring citizens. Throughout it all, the specter of environmental disaster looms large, just over the horizon.

While a continued rise in piracy will undoubtedly tend to affect consumers worldwide, the primary economic victims of increased piracy action will be the citizens of nations whose governments are unable, or unwilling, to adequately police their coastal waters. These nations will eventually see domestic businesses leave for other, safer regions with the inevitable result of increased local unemployment rates. The citizens in these nations will see particularly high prices for imported goods, as only the most expensive or well-equipped shipping companies will find it economically feasible to bring imports into dangerous waters. The costs of consumer goods will increase accordingly.

It seems clear that the solution to the piracy problem will not be found within the maritime industry itself—the economic loss to piracy is too minute to generate any real pressure on the industry to combat the threat. Indeed, the human cost in lives, injury, and safety far outstrips the economic losses. Governments, both individually and collectively, represent the only entities with both the motivation and the resources to effectively eradicate or, at least, decrease maritime piracy. Only through government intervention will the threat to both commerce and merchant mariners of all nations be eliminated.

Pirates, Terrorists, and Environmental Horrors

There is no question at all that the world has been most fortunate in so far avoiding an environmental disaster caused either indirectly by pirates or directly by terrorists. In this chapter, using the proposed International Maritime Bureau's broadened definition of piracy to encompass all terrorist acts committed on the water, we will attempt to include both species of marine criminals in the discussion of how they may adversely affect the environment.

Incidents reported in earlier chapters of this book included cases where crew members of ships were removed or disabled and their vessels continued without check to plow through crowded waters. The following section looks at these and other incidents from an environmental viewpoint.

SOME GRIM AND SCARY HISTORY

The potential for a major shipping disaster, without deliberate help from the human element, has always been present. Over the years, as cargoes have become more lethal, the danger to vessels, crew members, and people ashore has continued to grow.

Ships have a way of colliding with such things as docks, bridges, and each other. Loading and unloading dangerous cargo presents yet another major problem as shown by the Port Chicago, California, explosion during World War II and another at the Earle, New Jersey, Naval Ammunition Depot immediately after that conflict.

The modern examination of disasters, however, goes back to early in the century, specifically to 6 December 1917 and to Halifax, Nova Scotia.[1] The war was at its height in Europe and Halifax was among the most active Canadian ports handling military cargo destined for France.

On that morning, the *Imo,* a freighter carrying Red Cross supplies, was leaving Halifax and scheduled to join a convoy that was assembling outside the harbor. Another ship, the *Mont Blanc,* a freighter with a far less friendly cargo consisting of dynamite, benzene, and picric acid, was also to join the waiting convoy.

In order to reach the convoy assembly area, both ships had to transit a channel leading to the outer harbor. At approximately nine o'clock, in calm waters and with good visibility, the ships collided with Armageddonlike results. The explosion ripped down some three thousand homes in Halifax, killed four thousand people, and severely injured eight thousand more.

The subsequent investigation never revealed which of the ships was the cause of the collision as they moved down the channel on that horrible morning. The damage sustained by the environment, which undoubtedly occurred, was neither considered nor understood.

The possibility of in-port disaster is, unfortunately, an ever present one and it is made an even more serious concern by the fact that terrorists or pirates, as in the infamous and soon-to-be-mentioned case of the *Stolt Spur,* can create such horrendous devastation.

Another example of what can happen when bad things get together is the famous Texas City disaster.[2] Just after nine o'clock in the morning on 16 April 1947, a French freighter, the *Grandcamp,* was taking on a cargo of ammonium nitrate. A fire broke out in the hold of the ship and the first of several massive explosions occurred within minutes.

Docked alongside the ill-fated *Grandcamp* was another ship, already loaded with ammonium nitrate. To compound the problem, both ships were opposite a huge Monsanto chemical plant. In close proximity to the huge chemical works were oil refineries and warehouses filled with sulfur. One by one they ignited and exploded.

Flaming balls of hemp twine that had been stowed aboard the *Grandcamp* were blown out and over the city, setting new fires wherever they landed. It was a storehouse from hell.

Initial estimates put the dead at twelve hundred and the injured at fifteen thousand. Smoke emanating from the fire and explosions was a major killer. Breathing without a mask generally meant instantly seared lungs and a subsequent, horrible death.

On 19 April, a full two days after the explosions took place, a reporter for the *New York Times* wrote: "In the shadow of the raging fires a lone cow munched away at scrubby grass, no one to care for her milk. The only other moving thing in the torn land was a red apron that waved on a wash line in an abandoned backyard."[3]

RUNNING AGROUND

By 1967, environmental damage was on everyone's mind and it became an even more pointed issue in March of that year when the giant, Liberian-registered oil tanker *Torrey Canyon,* then one of the largest (one hundred twenty thousand tons) ships in the world, ran aground on the Seven Stones reef off England's southern coast.

Birds and fish suffocated in the black slime that was disgorged from the ship's innards and spread over an area that covered two hundred sixty square miles of ocean. The attempt to dissolve the oil with two and one-half thousand gallons of detergent only added to the ecological disaster.[4]

On 24 March 1989, another supertanker, the *Exxon Valdez,* ran aground in Prince William Sound, off Alaska. The resulting spill was approximately eleven million gallons of oil. About 12 percent of that amount sank to the bottom of the ocean. Almost half of the oil, broken down into various chemicals, was still floating ashore as late as 1993. Approximately eighteen hundred miles of shoreline were contaminated; about a half million birds and up to five thousand sea otters were killed.[5] Possible permanent ecological damage in the area may be the result of both the spill and subsequent cleanup operations.

There were no pirates or terrorists involved in these events. The potential for mischief is there, however, as ships carrying ever more lethal cargoes share the waterways of the globe seven days of the week and around the clock. It is a virtual certainty that these two elements, the maritime criminals and some kind of a ship, will be joined together in what may well become one of the greatest catastrophes ever experienced anywhere in terms of both human and environmental devastation.

The two primary dangers are that an unmanned ship will run aground or into something, possibly another vessel. The end result would largely depend on the ship or ships involved. If one or both are oil tankers, the fire and spill would be of major consequence. If one or both should happen to be carrying an explosive cargo, the probable result is even more a cause for significant concern.

The classic piracy definition is, perhaps, no better examined for its modern application than in the cases dealt with here. It is very hard to tell pirates from terrorists when they threaten to blow up a tanker unless they are given some money. The criminal threat to do exactly that aboard the previously mentioned *Stolt Spur,* at Santos, Brazil, is one example. Some twenty armed criminals seized the tanker, held the crew at gunpoint, and, while searching the ship for money and valuables, repeatedly threatened to blow up the vessel.[6]

The *Stolt Spur* was loaded with ethanol, a substance with a notoriously low flash point, which, obviously, does not take kindly to bullets. An explosion and fire would have involved several ships in the vicinity and resulting widespread chaos.

CROWDED WATERS

Obviously, the *Exxon Valdez* and the *Torrey Canyon* hold no monopoly on running aground any more than the ill-fated liners *Titanic, Andrea Doria,* and *Stockholm* or the freighters *Imo* and *Mont Blanc* had with collisions. Some locations are more prone to accidents, however.

The Malacca Strait has been the scene of numerous ship groundings and collisions during the past decade. In only the period from June to September 1992, there were four such incidents in that waterway. One involved a collision between two supertankers and a second between the tanker *Nagasaki Spirit* and a containership the *Ocean Blessing.* There were some reported oil spills but there is some belief that the latter event was caused by pirates.[7]

The danger and general level or risk when operating large ships during the best of weather in crowded waters is thus obvious. Add pirates (or terrorists) to the mix and the resulting risk level becomes virtually beyond measure.

Recalling the reported incidents from earlier chapters, the freighter *Nadia J.* was attacked by pirates off Nigeria on

8 November 1997 and the bridge was left unmanned for some fifteen minutes.[8] It is highly doubtful that the attacking pirates were aware that the channel in which the *Nadia J.* was sailing was one hundred meters wide and that the danger of running aground had to be relatively slight.

By comparison, the Phillip Channel, which goes from Indonesia to Singapore, is one of the most crowded waterways in the world and the danger of ship collision is very high. A pirate takeover, coupled with an unmanned bridge or a disembarked crew, virtually guarantees a collision and a very possible resulting economic and ecological disaster.

Should a spill occur here, the consequences will be major and would, if on the magnitude of the *Exxon Valdez* case, create significant problems for Singapore, Malaysia, and Indonesia. It has been speculated that a major oil spill would result in closing the channel to ship traffic and shutting down port operations in Singapore. These closures could continue for several months with resulting economic chaos in the area.

Additionally, the area is the site of intense fishing activity that would be seriously and immediately curtailed and, for an indefinite period, might prove to be a lost resource. The anticipated loss of marine life would be substantial as would be the case with rookeries and nestings. Intertidal organisms, planktonic and nektonic populations that are the food base for fish, would be even more seriously affected.[9]

TERRORISM AT SEA

As noted earlier in this book, it is the desire of the International Maritime Bureau (IMB) to broaden the definition of piracy. As currently provided by the United Nations Convention on the Law of the Sea (UNCLOS) of 1982, piracy consists of an illegal act committed on the high seas and thus beyond the jurisdiction of any nation-state.[10] The IMB, by contrast, seeks to define piracy as "an act of boarding any vessel with the intent to commit theft or any other crime and with the intent or capability to use force in the furtherance of that act."[11]

SOME TERRORIST EXAMPLES

There is little doubt that the most well-known example of maritime terrorism was that involving the *Achille Lauro,* which occurred on 17 October 1985 in the eastern Mediterranean. Terrorists belonging to the Palestine Liberation Front boarded the liner with fake identification papers and, of course, a number of weapons. Subsequently, they seized the ship, murdered a wheelchair-bound passenger, and threw his body into the sea.

Other incidents stand out. On 11 July 1988, the passenger ferry *City of Poros,* while sailing in Greek waters, was attacked by terrorists. Then, members of the Moro Islamic Liberation Front (MILF) attacked the freighter *Miguel Lujan* and the ferry *Leonara* on 29 April 1997, while both ships were in the harbor at Isabela in the Philippines.

There are other examples of this kind of maritime crime. The cargo ship *Morang Bong* was captured off Sri Lanka on 7 July 1998 by members of the revolutionary group known as the Tamil Tigers. The group quickly took full responsibility for the incident, which included the murder of a crew member.

The Tamil Tigers were also responsible for the 9 September 1997 attack on the *Cordiality,* a Chinese freighter that, again, was sailing off Sri Lanka. Rocket grenades were fired at the ship with the result that four crew members were killed. In 1997, while off Trincomalee, the bulk carrier *Athena* was attacked and the ship's engine room was damaged by a bomb.

Finally, on 1 June 1999, NBC News reported that an armed group of men had boarded a passenger ferry off Mexico's east coast earlier that day. There were unconfirmed reports that the attackers were from an unidentified terrorist organization. Whether terrorists or pirates these criminals were interested in money. They robbed the passengers but apparently no one was injured.[12]

MILITARY TERRORISTS

Military terrorism is another area where it is extremely difficult to separate terrorism from piracy. Ships sailing off Somalia have been attacked by maritime criminals who purport to be members of that country's coast guard. Admittedly, Somalia is a special case since it is a country (loosely defined) run by warlords who have no clue as to the basic principles of modern society.

The people who run Somalia are not alone in carrying out maritime crimes under a cloak of official sanction. It is probably true, however, that the most ambitious and aggressive of the military pirates/terrorists are those from the People's Republic of China.

In 1995, the freighter *Hye Mieko* was seized by Chinese officers while off Cambodia and taken to Shanwei, China, where the cargo was removed. Similarly, in October 1997, the containership *Vosa Carrier* was forcibly boarded by Chinese soldiers and sailed to the port of Hui Lai. A ransom was demanded and paid and the cargo was seized.

One of the problems is that Chinese military units are, at least unofficially, encouraged to be self-sufficient. The result is that Chinese commanders and their crews, dressed in camouflage fatigues and with their boats flying the flag of the Peoples Republic of China, ply international waters in search of potential victims.

PROTECTING THE CARGO

There can be no doubt that the best defense against pirates, and to some degree at least, against terrorists, starts on the shore and with shipping agents. Only those who have good reputations and a sound knowledge of local authorities and how to deal with them should be selected. Such knowledge can sometimes be critically important and there are a lot of examples to prove it.

In February 1997, pirates dressed as members of the Somalian coast guard boarded a freighter, *Clove,* and demanded money. In May 1996, pirates dressed as port officials boarded the freighter *Porer* and subsequently stole money from the ship's safe. On 16 January 1996, pirates disguised as ordinary passengers (but hiding shotguns) seized the ferry *Avrasya* in the waters off Trabzon, Turkey. The pirates finally surrendered to authorities after lengthy hostage negotiations. The log carrier *Nandu Arrow,* while in port at Surabaya, Indonesia, on 18 January 1997 was boarded by several men who claimed to be stevedores. They were able to break into the ship's central stores and steal a variety of spare parts.

The idea of boarding a ship in disguise in order to commit crime is not a new one. On 14 March 1990, several men dressed as customs officers boarded a freighter, *Eastern Galaxy,* that was being loaded at Isabel in the Philippines. Unfortunately for them, they were discovered before completing their criminal venture.

Any documents that list a ship's cargo must always be tightly guarded. Despite the fact that some pirates are happy to steal paint and rope, there is more money to be made when fencing electronic equipment and other expensive items. If shore-based criminals can identify cargoes of value and, furthermore, identify the specific boxes in which such cargo has been placed on containerships, the easier it is to steal.

In May 1996, armed pirates boarded the containership *San Marino* off Santos, Brazil. They broke open twenty-two containers, opened ten of them, and stole from just two. In

March of that year, again off Brazil, five armed pirates boarded the containership *Vogtland,* broke into five containers, and stole computer parts.

Breaking into containers is not a skill limited to pirates off Brazil. On 8 January 1997, pirates boarded the *Mumbai Bay,* which was anchored at Colombo, India, and opened two containers.

PROTECTING THE CREW AND THE SHIP

Protection of cargo is important but it pales before providing protection for the crew members and for the ship itself. Experts in such matters, in this case, the members of the Maritime Safety Committee of the IMO, start with the point that before every sailing, the officers and crew must be aware of antipiracy procedures, signals that will be sounded, and who will be responsible for doing what if and when pirates appear.

The antipiracy plan should provide a secure place for the crew members to gather, one that has been prepared to contain emergency radio equipment and survival gear.

But the principal consideration is to try to keep pirates off the ship in the first place. All means of access to a ship must be sealed off with, for example, portholes closed.

Illumination of the surrounding area is important. Pirates, like commonplace burglars on land, are not fond of working in well-lit areas. Maritime security experts, however, do suggest that ships sailing in areas that are known to be "high-hazard" ones as far as pirates are concerned, should only light the waters around the vessel. Attackers will, in such cases, have no knowledge of what may be met on deck. Again, like commonplace burglars, pirates do not like surprises.

WHILE IN PORT

Classic piracy occurs on the high seas, but modern pirates can and do attack ships that are within harbors or just outside of them. While it is easy, if not smug, to say that such attacks, for the most part, occur in the ports of Asia and South America, harbors in the United States are not immune. In July 1997, the *Vanderpool Express* was boarded at Miami and eight crew members were murdered. In January 1998, the *Shandeline,* also berthed in Miami, was boarded. Preventive measures include increased radio-equipped security patrols, extensive lighting, and a sound knowledge of which local authorities are to be called and their location.

WHILE AT SEA

Illumination is, again, a highly recommended piracy deterrent, if wisely employed. The use of the ship's whistle can also be helpful through its ability to gain attention (and possibly assistance) from other ships and from local authorities that may be in the area.

Ships that have entered waters known to be favorite hunting grounds (high-hazard areas) for pirates have an extra burden. It is recommended that, as opposed to remaining in anchorages where attacks can be made by pirates with a much higher degree of ease, ships should sail from twenty to fifty miles offshore where their vulnerability is far more limited.

Whether sailing offshore or on the high seas, ships should have their water hoses charged. Blasts from high-pressure hoses have proven successful on more than one ship in deterring pirates who were attempting to board. Being washed overboard is something that even the most water-tested pirate does not relish even though it may come as part of the territory for a marine criminal.

Pirates who attempt to board a moving ship are a more adventurous breed than their counterparts who sneak aboard while a ship is at anchor or while it is alongside a dock. Generally, waterborne pirates will approach a ship from the stern—sometimes even when a vessel is moving as fast as seventeen knots—using a small boat. As in days of old, grappling hooks are used and the pirates climb up the ropes to the deck. If they can get that far, they have the element of surprise in their favor. If that element is backed up by firepower, the pirates will be in control.

If a ship is under way and pirates are seen, the first thing that is recommended by experts is to increase speed and keep lights on the intruders. The procedure known by mariners as "wagging the tail" has also proved to be an excellent deterrent and consists of rapidly moving the ship's stern back and forth.

Meanwhile, of course, the hoses must be ready and the radio must be used to communicate the fact that pirates are attacking.

More Lethal, Less Passive Means

The crew of the yacht *Poloflat,* while sailing through the Red Sea during November 1998, was attacked by pirates but beat them off through the use of homemade Molotov cocktails. These devices are generally created by using a glass bottle filled with gasoline. A rag (or wick) is then stuffed in the neck of the bottle and is lit just before the bottle is thrown. Properly used, Molotov cocktails can stop tanks on land and it seems obvious that, in this case, the people aboard the yacht knew how to make and throw them. Other yacht owners have used rifles, shotguns, and flare pistols to defend themselves against seaborne marauders, with effective results. Luck, at least as much as skill, can play a big part in favorably resolving such incidents.

Tear gas has proven to be yet another option. The always-present problem with tear gas, as it is with self-protection devices such as Mace, is that the wind can render the gas useless or, worse yet, make the user the victim. The issue of armed force to meet pirate attacks is still open to serious debate and is covered in detail in chapter 7 ("Solutions").

Of course, deterrence in the form of punishment must be considered. In this regard, the actions taken by the United Arab Emirates in 1989 may be instructive. Two pirates were tried, convicted, and then sentenced under Muslim law. The sentence imposed on each of the two men was the amputation of one arm and one leg on opposite sides of the body.[13] In a less dramatic, but perhaps equally effective move, the Philippine government reinstated the death penalty for piracy in February 1993.[14]

PIRATE WEAPONS

There are, it seems, as many types of weapons used by pirates, as there are pirates themselves. Nuts and bolts were thrown at the tanker *Rita* by pirates off Kandla, India, in May 1997.[15] Swords were the pirate's weapons of choice when attacking the bulk carrier *Great Calm* off Taraan, Panjang, in March 1997.[16] A slingshot was used to wound a watchman at Bangkok Bay, Thailand, in 1997.[17] Stones were thrown at a watchman by attacking pirates in 1995.[18] At the other end of the weapons spectrum, pirates are well known for their use of everything from automatic rifles such as the M-16 and AK-47 to rocket launchers, grenade launchers, and mortars.

POST ATTACK

Mariners are constantly urged by organizations such as the IMB to report piracy and terrorist incidents as soon as possible. These reports should be filed with the relevant law enforcement agency, the shipowner, and the IMB. The reports should be made whatever the location of the incident and without regard to the success or failure of the attackers. The time, place, means of attack, number of attackers, and measures used to repel boarders must be included in every postattack report. Not only does this kind of information provide a means of curtailing piracy, it serves to show the dangers faced today at sea from maritime crime.

One problem that has been faced by the IMB and law enforcement authorities has been that masters have often faced considerable delays after filing reports in some ports of the world. A second issue appears to be that there is a cultural, as well as commercial, reticence on the part of some officers and shipping companies to file reports.

PIRATES AND TERRORISTS COMPARED

It is important here to note the differences involved in deterring pirates and terrorists who operate in a maritime environment. They are clearly, despite attempts to make their nefarious acts punishable under a broader definition, totally separate maritime criminals, and for any considerations of deterrence must be treated that way.

Pirates might be dissuaded, for example, from taking over a ship by using charged fire hoses. Terrorists won't be. They will come armed to the teeth and well trained. Only a military force will be capable of fighting and defeating them. There is also the fact that terrorists would generally board a ship as was done with the *Achille Lauro,* often with the help of confederates already aboard. Pirates have done that as well, as in the numerous cases already cited. But despite that, pirates can be handled successfully by most regular police authorities once the criminals are discovered.

Finally, with passengers or an entire port at risk, if the seized ship were a tanker or a vessel loaded with some explosive cargo (remember the ammonium nitrate at Texas City), there is little that can be done in such a case except to negotiate and hope for a substantial amount of luck. Of course, if the particular brand of terrorists are intent only on making a political statement and dying for their cause, the issue becomes one of disaster management.

There is an essential difference between pirates and terrorists in terms of the current law. It is that terrorists who commit crimes at sea are motivated by political ends and that pirates are motivated by money.

While there are arguments that can be mounted for and against the broadened definition of piracy as promoted by the International Maritime Bureau and that effectively make terrorists into pirates and punishable as such, there are serious distinctions between pirates and marine terrorists. Pirates are now, and historically have always been, engaged in a criminal pursuit for profit. Terrorists do what they do to make a statement for a political cause. Pirates want to live to enjoy the fruits of their (albeit nefarious) labors. Terrorists are willing (or want) to die to prove a point.

While antipiracy measures of any kind, whether proactive or reactive, can be considered and debated, terrorism and terrorists represent a different kind of enemy. They will rarely be subjected to being washed overboard with charged fire hoses.

And terrorists who will choose to attack ships or will use ships as a means of achieving destruction in a port city are of particular concern. A look back on the accidentally caused disasters at Halifax and Texas City can provide what may be a relatively minor idea of what well-armed terrorists can achieve today by cold-blooded and sophisticated design.

Government efforts around the world can be mounted to deal with the aftermath of a terrorist attack (although no one knows how well that can be done if the attack is either of the nuclear or biological form). And although postattack criminal investigations and prosecutions may track down and provide well-deserved lethal sentences for perpetrators, the damage will have been done and the dead and wounded may be beyond count.

In truth, the most effective antiterrorist weapon is a well-organized, well-financed, and effectively operated international intelligence program. There is no room for error.

As far back as the late 1970s, one terrorism expert had declared that one terrorist with one nuclear weapon in a suitcase could take out Manhattan from the Battery to 14th Street, river to river.

Given the increased lethality of terrorism, the danger has been expanded to include biological and chemical weapons. The net result is a continuing threat to the air we breathe, to the water we drink, and to life itself both through instant attack and its long-term environmental consequences. There is nothing more sobering than that.

Solutions

I t is usually a good idea to examine a problem and its causes before attempting to devise solutions. When one tries to find a way of reducing the growing threat of modern day maritime crime (to include piracy on the high seas, armed robbery in territorial waters, and terrorism), the value of that idea is certainly not diminished.

Historic Reasons

Piracy, as noted in the beginning of this book, has been around for a very long time. The causes are both politics and ordinary greed. The results, in any case, are criminal. For purposes of clarity in dealing with this issue, the concept of privateering, which was state sanctioned, is not part of this analysis although it will be subsequently mentioned in a different frame of reference, that of armed self-defense.

One reason for piracy, in terms of political factors, is the existence throughout history of laws that have been unpopular because they were designed to restrict trade. This was true in the case of British North America and the infamous Navigation Acts as well as with the Chinese and Japanese attempts to control trade beginning in the fourteenth century.

In every case where laws were enacted to restrict trade, two things occurred. The first was the appearance of pirates who could seize desired goods on the high seas and the second was the appearance of the people on shore who could buy the goods and make them available to the market.

A second reason for piracy was, as mentioned earlier, pure and simple greed. Like most criminals, pirates of every kind are highly opportunistic.

These forces persist in modern times. Where the pirates of bygone days knew there was a ready market for spices and silks, those of today recognize the market for VCRs and camcorders.

EFFECTS OF DEFINITIONS

There are, as we have already noted, several accepted definitions of piracy, the classic one stating that it is a violent crime for private ends committed on the high seas.[1]

Expanded definitions of piracy as desired by some organizations such as the International Maritime Bureau (IMB) do increase the number of reported (and reportable) incidents of piracy. The broader definition, as formulated by the IMB, provides that piracy "is the act of boarding any vessel with the intent to commit theft or other crime, with the capability to use force in furtherance of the act."[2]

Because the use of such a definition will serve to increase the number of piracy incidents, some have leveled major criticisms at the use of a definition that makes an admittedly bad problem even worse by including as pirates a lot of street thugs.[3]

Indeed, piracy, through the broadened definition, will include an armed robbery committed aboard a passenger liner that is docked on Manhattan's west side, where the perpetrator has gained access to the ship by walking aboard and has a screwdriver or pocket knife as a weapon. It is highly doubtful that the New York City Police Department will really consider such a miscreant to be a pirate, but the statistics published by the IMB will reflect him (or her) as one.

ANOTHER PROBLEM

Once piracy is accepted by broad definition to include a variety of criminal acts committed on any vessel on any body of water, a single good solution to the problem is going to be much harder to find. When piracy is of the classic variety—that is to say, conducted on the high seas and excepting maritime terrorism—the issue remains one that can be dealt with by any sovereign state.

Having made these prefatory comments, we will now examine the available solutions to the piracy and maritime crime problem (regardless of the definitions) and leave the reader to apply them as desired.

TERRITORIAL WATERS

The threat from piracy, again using that term to embrace the activities of armed robbers who board a ship or boat that is docked or anchored, is a very serious and sometimes deadly one.

In most cases (and particularly at the docks and in the anchorages of Brazil), the attacks occur in the early hours of the morning. The boarders do their best not to alert the crew and thus deny the opportunity for any alarm to be sounded. One or more crew members are often taken hostage in order to gain access to crew quarters and to the ship's safe. Usually, the vessel's communications system is disabled to delay the report of the assault. Finally, the crew is robbed and, if the ship is a container vessel, several boxes (often specific ones that have been obviously identified by on-shore confederates), are broken into and some or all of the contents are removed. The desired goods are then off-loaded and the pirates depart.

In the vast majority of cases, this kind of piracy falls within the province of the police to both prevent and solve. However, experts in the port and ship security field have recommended several helpful steps. The first is to have a prevention or antiattack plan that includes increased detection and surveillance of the ship and its surroundings; crew-awareness training relevant to boarding procedures used by pirates; and adoption of special radio and alarm procedures to be used when an attack occurs. Additionally, ships are advised to avoid docks and anchorages where attacks are known to have occurred and to remain under way for as long as possible as an alternative to dropping anchor.[4] But such procedures, as helpful as they are, cover only one part of a highly complex problem.

PORT SECURITY

Unless a port (and that term as used here includes docks, anchorages, and oil terminals such as Santos and Alemona, in Brazil) is first kept and then maintained as a secure environment, crime will be a major problem and a growing one.

While Brazil and Haiti are the current worst examples of port security, those locations have no monopoly on crime and corruption. For at least a decade, attacks (some of them particularly vicious and resulting in casualties to include fatalities) have occurred at docks, anchorages, and offshore waters in Nigeria, Benin, Sierra Leone, Liberia, Bangladesh, Sri Lanka, and the Philippines to provide just a sample of international trouble spots.[5]

Again, the motivation of both armed robbers and ordinary thieves is greed. Whether the items stolen have a significant value in the grey market or are mundane items like paint, rope, and hand tools that can simply be sold right in the waterfront district's hardware stores, there still must be a receiver (a fence) who will buy the stolen property for subsequent resale.

The key, then, is to keep the law enforcement pressure on the waterfront and on the fences. And the first step is to do it the old-fashioned way, through a uniformed police presence in strength. This kind of "showing the flag" has to be supported by a continuing program of undercover activity, dedicated and professional surveillance, and collection and analysis of intelligence that is shared by law enforcement and military agencies that are involved in the program.

Corruption on the waterfront, including everyone from the watchmen and stevedores, through their supervisors and the union managements into the government agencies (including law enforcement and military personnel), is both possible and (where there is a lot of money) probable. What is needed to counter that problem is a hard core of trusted professionals whose job it is to keep track of the bad guys and to ensure that the good guys stay that way.

If port security is attained through tough land-based investigation, enforcement, and prosecution, profits from maritime crime on the waterfront will drop because the risks will simply be too high.

Clearly, prevention on the ships and aggressive law enforcement on the docks, in the harbors, and in territorial waters must be an integrated process with the ultimately desired end being to make crime unprofitable.

ARMED ROBBERY AT SEA

While piracy (or less glamorously termed, "street scum armed robbery"), which occurs at docks and within territorial waters, is one thing, classic piracy on the high seas has other dimensions. It presents far greater difficulties in reaching a viable solution and has a very high potential in some scenarios for the creation of serious international incidents.

As discussed in chapter 4, attacks on the high seas and those directed at ships that are under way in territorial waters have principally been occurring in Southeast Asia and off the coasts of Africa. Such attacks have included those where pirates were armed with mortars, rocket launchers, and heavy automatic weapons. In one case, off Somalia, a tanker, the *Helena,* was fired on by pirates with grenade launchers.[6] In another incident, which occurred in Manila Bay, pirates fired a rocket at the ocean liner *Sky Princess.*[7]

As with attacks made by armed robbers in territorial waters and in ports, the early morning hours are the favored time for pirates to attack ships that are under way on the high seas. Usually, these attackers have a sound knowledge of ships and have approached vessels moving as fast as seventeen knots. The pirates use ropes and grappling hooks to reach the deck. From that point, the procedures used are similar to those employed by armed robbers in the ports. The high-seas pirates, however, do seem more violence oriented than their inshore counterparts and are generally better armed. After robbing the crew and taking whatever they can from the ship's cargo, the pirates usually lock the crew members in their quarters. The pirates then depart, leaving the vessel moving without anyone on the bridge. In other incidents, some or all of the crew members have been taken off the ship and held hostage.[8]

There is another difference in the methods of attack used by some pirates in Southeast Asia. Assaults have occurred in broad daylight and have begun with the pirates opening fire on a targeted vessel with rocket-propelled grenades, heavy machine guns, and mortars for the purpose of stopping it.[9]

MARITIME TERRORISM

The essential elements that separate piracy on the high seas and armed robbery that occurs in port from terrorism are two. The first is that violence is the expected (and desired) result of terrorism and is the reason for the act itself. The second is that the motivation for terrorism is, in many (if not most) cases, either religious or political. Recent examples include an attack on 29 April 1997 by members of the Moro Islamic Liberation Front (MILF), who machine gunned a cargo ship and a passenger ferry at Isabela in the Philippines, and several incidents in which Tamil rebels attacked vessels off Sri Lanka. One attack, directed at the bulk carrier *Panama,* occurred on 9 September 1997 at Sri Lanka and resulted in thirty-three people killed and another seventeen wounded.[10] The 1985 attack on the passenger liner *Achille Lauro* is probably the most well-known example of maritime terrorism.

While port security and crew awareness training will always have a beneficial effect, the value of these factors when up against terrorism, at least in its most lethal forms, will have minimal positive results. The key to the prevention of terrorism is good intelligence and multinational cooperation. And while port security is often a major local law enforcement effort, effective counterterrorism in all of its various dimensions must involve the highest levels of national resources and commitment.

ACTION PLANNING

We have discussed scenarios and the means to prevent maritime crime in port and at sea. The inevitable question must arise, however, regarding what to do if the pirates or the terrorists show up. A discussion of antipiracy measures can also be found in chapter 6.

As noted, trying to create solutions to the problem of piracy on the high seas is more difficult than dealing with crime on the harbors and rivers of the world. However, the bottom line for the crew of any ship or boat, regardless of its location is whether or not to resist attack and, if the first alternative is chosen, how to do it. There is a decided difference of opinion on the whole question of resistance, which runs the spectrum of vessels from huge cargo ships to pleasure boats. Finally, there are the legal consequences of resisting pirates, both at sea and within a foreign state's territorial waters including while at dockside.

THE NONLETHAL APPROACH

If prevention fails, whether at a dock, while anchored, or under way either in territorial waters or on the high seas, there are some measures that are suggested by experts that could help ward off pirates. These measures include sounding alarms and using the ship's whistle and, when under way, executing a variety of evasive maneuvers such as causing the stern to move rapidly back and forth, a procedure that is sometimes referred to as "wagging the tail."[11] Effectively, however, the only "offensive" action that seems to be approved is the use of already charged fire hoses against the pirates in the hope that this action will cool their felonious intent or, hopefully, will cause them to be washed overboard into waters infested by hungry sharks.

Once the pirates are aboard, it is a majority recommendation that they should be accommodated, with crew safety being the foremost consideration.[12] The basic advice provided by some (not all) experts is the same that we have heard about what to do when confronted by a mugger on the street or even by a burglar in the living room and that is to let the criminal have what he wants, hope that he won't then decide to kill you and, after he has left, call the police.

A problem with the idea of not aggravating the criminal marauders is that they are using increasingly violent methods. And that, almost inevitably, means that more and more crew members are going to be killed and wounded regardless of how the pirates are accommodated.

THE ARMED RESPONSE

The choice of whether or not to resist attack on the water is a far easier one to make for the pleasure boater. A visit to a major pleasure-boat harbor on the East Coast was highly instructive in this regard. One very large yacht operated by a professional crew and owned by a wealthy Dutch gem dealer would not be a good selection for attack by the most dedicated pirates or terrorists. It reportedly has a .50-caliber machine gun and a rocket launcher aboard. How this kind of arsenal can be acquired and moved around the world without running afoul of somebody's law is an open question. The fact remains, however, that the boat is so armed. Its crew members are alleged to be former Rhodesian soldiers who are well trained in the use of the weapons. Clearly, this particular boat owner has made his choice between nonlethal and lethal defense.

He is not alone by any stretch of the imagination. Rifles, handguns, and twelve-gauge stainless steel shotguns are kept on a lot of boats. One law enforcement official in the Caribbean said of that: "Remember, even with a radio, you're out on a very big ocean all alone. If I were a pleasure boat operator—I'd be armed out there, too."[13]

But, even among pleasure boaters, there is a different view. One boater—interestingly enough with a law enforcement background—said that the only "weapon" he carries on the boat is a flare gun, "with a lot of flares."

In terms of the pleasure boater, the choices seem to be based on the same kind of thinking that accompanies home defense. Are there children on board? Can the weapons be maintained safely? If they have to be used, is there sufficient weapons knowledge and familiarity? The answers to these kinds of questions all become part of the decision about having weapons on board and, of course, using them.

The decision faced by the professionals in the maritime industry is not quite so easy.

TWO VIEWS

The International Maritime Bureau (IMB), the Seamen's Institute, and the International Shipping Federation have gone on record in opposition to the idea of arming ships and crews against pirates or terrorists.

In a recent address, Douglas Stevenson, executive director of the Seamen's Church Institute, said:

> Some commentators have suggested that ship's crews should be armed to protect themselves against piracy. (Historically, ship's crews were expected to protect their ship and cargo from pirates.) I can tell you that from what we hear from seafarers, they do not favor this approach. They are not trained for this and they do not want to raise the level of violence that this would entail. We agree, believing that arming merchant ships would raise the level of violence and further jeopardize crew's safety. Our advice to seafarers is that they do not resist pirates, that their property is not worth risking their life to protect. Their personal property is probably protected by insurance. And, from the shipowners prospective, [*sic*] given the choice between paying crewmembers for their property taken by pirates and paying death and injury claims resulting from attempts to protect the property, most shipowners would rather pay the relatively low personal property claims.[14]

But, as noted earlier, pirate attacks are becoming more vicious. While there is an argument for the nonviolent approach, there is an equally good one for taking the opposite view. Pirates don't want to die, either, and terrorists (some of whom do) will not be dissuaded from pulling the trigger because they are faced with accommodating behavior.

And yet, one must note the fact that most crew members do not sign on with any desire to become part of any ship's armed guard. Most of these people, first of all, have no training in police or paramilitary operations and have no interest in getting it. Crew member duties are hard and hazardous enough without adding combat to the job description.

Shipowners, insurance companies, and maritime unions have the same view. Not only does the problem arise about having crew members killed or wounded, but also there is always the possibility of someone being shot by accident during a training drill or even during an actual attack when some guys with black hats try to board the ship.

Training of crew members, even if desired, represents a problem. Today's ship crews are small and may speak, collectively, five or six languages. Add to this the potential for liability, and the reasoning for the idea of not wanting regular ship crews to fight it out with pirates does make a great deal of sense.

But there is another view, espoused by one Capt. Philip Cheek in an unpublished essay, where he proposes that "suspicion alone, that a vessel is carrying among her crew, half a dozen trained killers would have a snowball effect. It would probably only need one surprise shoot-out, say off Santos, or Hong Kong, killing every boarder, to send out the right message."[15]

While this view is not currently embraced by the majority of those engaged in combating piracy, positions may radically change as pirate violence continues to increase. If and when a real bloodbath occurs on some merchant vessel, it will be no surprise to find a lot of people changing their minds, not about arming crew members, but about fighting back with weapons other than fire hoses.

One example of that change is already said to have occurred and quite possibly as a result of the *Sky Princess* episode. It is reported, but could not be confirmed, that at least one passenger ship line has quietly placed former military personnel (Gurkas were specifically mentioned) on its liners to provide security. It is, quite understandably, very difficult to get even general information on something like this, let alone any specifics about it.

But there are some very interesting points that arise from the possibility (actually the probability, given the nature of the information source) of such passenger ship armings. The first is that some of those who have opposed arming vessels have based their opposition on the point that such ships could be considered privateers. And the second is the objection to generally arming merchant ships because of the fact that if it were necessary to take action against maritime criminals in a foreign port or in territorial waters, the armed force aboard the ship might have no protection from the statutes of the foreign state. It is possible to deal with both of these objections together.

If tankers, bulk carriers, and containerships, because they are prepared to defend themselves, can be considered as privateers, that must also be said of passenger liners, which are also merchant ships differentiated from the others only because they are carrying human cargo. Indeed, carried to the extreme, the privateer label could also be applied to oceangoing pleasure boats with arms aboard that are being carried for self-defense. If armed self-defense is to become equated with privateering, we have reached a sad point in our legal experience.

While, as mentioned previously, crew members do not sign on merchant vessels to become part-time military or law enforcement personnel, neither do they have any intent to become victims of violent crime. The pressure for their protection will come from the unions, if nowhere else, if piracy acts of every kind and wherever committed, become increasingly violent.

A MULTINATIONAL APPROACH

There have been suggestions that providing at least some merchant ships with professionally trained and armed personnel (presumably marines or special forces) could be done under the auspices of the United Nations or through some other kind of international agreement.

This would be a good idea if it would work. The problem is that reaching an agreement on something like this is never easy at the UN and even when it is there is always the overriding question of who will pay for the project. Most of the nation-state members of the UN are not, after all, direct beneficiaries of ocean commerce and they would balk at having to pay anything to make it safe, or to provide military personnel for the program.

An alternative course is the formation of a non-UN (but nonetheless multilateral) group of states with a major maritime interest, possibly because their nationals represent a significant percentage of crew members. Specially trained and well-equipped personnel provided by these member nations could be placed at the last minute on selected ships and would be kept separate from the crew. Their task would be to protect the ship from pirates acting under the motivation of terrorism or simple greed. It might be an added consideration to have a video camera operator serve with each of these groups for the purpose of making a complete record of any pirate attack and the presumed result. In a takeoff on

Captain Cheek's proposal, a videotape showing what can happen to pirates, to include those dead on deck covered with blood or floating in the water, would have the desired, and chilling, effect, particularly when released to the media.

The existence and use of such a force and its hoped-for success in curtailing high-seas piracy could also positively impact the kind of criminal activity that occurs in the highly dangerous ports and territorial waters of the world. But there are problems to be considered and overcome before such a solution can be implemented.

THE SMALL "P" PIRATES

Given the fact that many of the reported violent pirate incidents take place aboard ships that are at anchorages or alongside docks, the solution to this aspect of the problem, as well as that of maritime crime on the high seas, requires both international action and cooperation.

The probability is small that all (or even most) of the nations of the world would relish any merchant ship entering their territorial waters with an armed force aboard. And, they would like it even less if such a force went into action against criminals assaulting it in a harbor. Indeed, without agreements to cover whatever national ports a protected merchant ship will enter, the forces aboard may find themselves in legal difficulties when acting in their own self-defense.

There is yet another point to consider when discussing the arming of merchant ships and even assuming that the force involved was a disciplined, military one that had the needed blessings conferred on it by an international body. If such forces were to be deployed at the last possible moment on selected ships, what would happen if that vessel were to be attacked somewhere in the South China Sea by a patrol boat manned by members of the People's Republic of China? The possibility of such a confrontation, at least since the current piracy activities of that government's military have begun to increase, is not a remote one.

It has been observed that, on several occasions, the pirates of Southeast Asia are flying the Chinese flag. It is equally true that since 1995, several incidents have occurred in which armed and uniformed Chinese have boarded ships on the high seas and then forced the vessels to sail to Chinese ports where the cargo was off-loaded.[16]

What would the protectors of such a ship be expected to do in such a situation? It would not be unreasonable for them to engage the attackers but if that occurred, the diplomatic flurry would be interesting to see. Despite the diplomats, one would have to say that the attackers got what they deserved. Crime should not go unpunished, even if a national government is committing it.

The need is for collective action on the part of the international community to include discussions aimed at resolving problems that may arise when lethal force is used against armed maritime criminals.

During mid-1998, two new counterpiracy possibilities were announced. One is a satellite-based tracking system that, once installed on a ship, tells monitors if there is any deviation from course. A second approach is to link such satellite tracking to a privately financed rapid response team composed of British special forces personnel that will seek to recover the ship along with, presumably, the cargo and crew. As might be expected, this antipiracy initiative has proven to be controversial.

CAVEAT

Military and law enforcement organizations are only as good as the governments that operate them. If a government is populated by corrupt, lazy, and inefficient officials, it is a certainty that the military and law enforcement personnel operating under it will mirror such proclivities. And if such governments cannot or will not effectively seek to stop the "small p" pirates whom we have here generally categorized as street scum thugs, then maritime crime in the ports and in anchorages around the world will not be significantly reduced.

OTHER RESPONSES

If there is to be any viable hope of reducing the threat and problem of modern piracy, the overarching requirement is teamwork that must have the continuing active involvement of ship operators, shipowners, shippers, labor unions, and governments around the world. While it is true that some nations are landlocked, it is equally true that there are few (if any) places in the world where there is no beneficial effect to be found—albeit indirectly—from ocean commerce. As a result, there is a good case to be made for the fact that high-seas crime has such a significantly high level of international importance that it must be fought by all nations on a concerted basis. The activities of the International Maritime Organization (IMO), a component part of the United Nations, have already proved valuable. This organization, through its Maritime Safety Committee, issues quarterly reports of all piracy incidents, broken down into geographic areas, and contains a detailed analysis of the piracy situation on a worldwide basis.[17]

The role of the International Maritime Bureau (IMB), as part of the International Chamber of Commerce, is also a critical one. Surely, the creation by the group of the Regional Piracy Centre (RPC), based at Kuala Lumpur, Malaysia, is a major factor in the battle against maritime crime. Founded at the suggestion of the IMB in 1995, the RPC is financed by contributions made by shipping companies and insurance carriers. Among its continuing activities are the providing of reports of suspicious movements of vessels and assisting law enforcement agencies in their antipiracy efforts.

Ongoing human-oriented programs as sponsored by the Seamen's Church Institute and the International Transport Worker's Federation have proven highly valuable in assisting crew members in dealing with the psychological and physical trauma that accompanies pirate attack. The labor unions must recognize that their members are the ones who are personally being victimized and face the greatest physical, one-to-one danger from pirates, however they are defined and wherever they are found.

The International Federation of Ship Owners, along with the Baltic and International Maritime Council (BIMCO), an industry group that represents more than 55 percent of the world's merchant shipping fleet and is a clearinghouse for reported incidents, have also been increasingly active in providing a wide variety of programs to combat piracy both on the high seas and in the ports.

Ship operators have, in some ways, contributed to the piracy problem because of a lack of interest in reporting incidents. There are three reasons for this attitude. The first is that few ship operators want to be known as having been the target for pirates. It's bad for business. A second reason is that when incidents are reported, some port authorities have been known to delay ship departures while conducting an investigation. This, too, is bad for business. A third reason has to do with concern over increased insurance rates charged by the ocean marine insurance carriers.[18]

MARINE INSURERS

The insurance companies are, in all fairness, heavily involved in trying to solve the piracy and overall maritime crime problem. Eventually, losses suffered as a result of such criminal activity will be borne by them whenever the standard "free of Capture and Seizure" clause is waived by providing desired coverage to an assured. The clause, unless waived, excludes piracy from the perils that the standard ocean marine coverage provides. It reads:

> Warranted free of capture, seizure, arrest, restraint or detainment, and the consequences thereof or any attempt thereat; also from the consequences of hostilities or warlike operations, whether there by a declaration of war or not. . . . Further warranted free from the consequences of civil war, revolution, rebellion, insurrection, or civil strife arising therefrom, or *piracy*.[19] [The emphasis is provided.]

For purposes of historical interest, the far more famous insurance clause, which was an integral part of every policy issued by the underwriters of Lloyd's of London, and which did cover piracy, reads as follows:

> Touching the adventures and perils which we the assurers are contented to bear and do take upon us in the voyage: they are of the seas, men-of-war, fire, enemies, *pirates,* rovers, thieves, jettisons, letters of *mart* and countermart, surprisals, takings at sea, arrests, restraints, and detainments of all kings, princes, and people, of whatever nation, condition, or quality soever, barratry of the master and mariners, and of all other perils, losses, and misfortunes, that have or shall come to the hurt, detriment, or damage of the said goods and merchandises, and ship, &c., or any part thereof.[20] [The emphasis is supplied.]

In specific terms, the insurance underwriters not only have a vested interest in oceans and territorial waters that are relatively free from criminals, they have the vast resources and not insignificant political clout, even on an international basis, to help make that desire a reality. Experts provided by the insurance companies can provide help to prevent maritime crime and money for equipment and the training of personnel. Finally, the insurance companies have the contacts and expertise that will help to create and maintain continuing media interest in the maritime crime problem.

THE MEDIA

Pirates, like all other criminals since the beginning of recorded history, have trouble functioning with the lights turned on them. In this case, the light is that cast by unrelenting media attention with resulting public and, of course, official attention.

And the media have a major responsibility to turn on the switch and shine lights into the dark corners of the world of modern piracy and all of its land-based support systems. The public needs to be educated. From experience gained in the preparation of this book, that process has a long way to go. One cocktail party will be enough for the reader to test that conclusion.

Most people, when the word piracy is mentioned, identify it with international copyright violations, not with armed criminals boarding a ship. A pirate is still largely thought of in terms of Captain Kidd or his fictional counterpart, Captain Hook. Based on this level of awareness, real piracy is dead and the rest is entertainment.

In the absence of some truly horrific piracy-related event, however, the interest of the media can only be maintained through the concentrated efforts of key groups with a vested interest in successfully targeting maritime crime.

MULTINATIONAL COOPERATION

International cooperation, aside from the question of arming ships, is a vital element of any serious program aimed at bringing maritime crime, in all its aspects, under effective control. The previously mentioned activities of the

International Maritime Organization at the United Nations must be maintained and expanded relevant to piracy and related criminal activities.

The efforts of individual nations are also clearly important, particularly in terms of sharing intelligence on maritime crime and its perpetrators. Examples of this kind of ongoing activity are the programs conducted by the U.S. Department of State through the Overseas Advisory Council and the Marine Operations Division of Revenue Canada.

In the Caribbean, some planning efforts have been undertaken by the countries of Central America to coordinate antipiracy programs. These efforts, which began with a conference of naval officers from various nations at Tegucigalpa, Honduras, in October 1992, have not been subject to effective assessment.

And in that area of the world where piracy and other maritime crimes are generally the most numerous and most ferocious, namely Southeast Asia, there have been attempts to combat the problem through some multinational efforts. One has been the development of an agreement between Indonesia and the Philippines to permit the hot pursuit of pirates into the latter's territorial waters. Indonesia has also become a party to an agreement with both Malaysia and Singapore to create and operate a sophisticated radar surveillance system to monitor waterways in that area. In addition, Indonesia has entered into agreements with Singapore to establish antipiracy naval patrols in the Phillip Channel and the Singapore Straits. Similarly, Indonesia and Malaysia have created a program to provide increased security in the Straits of Malacca.

CONCLUSIONS

Achieving a sharp public, industry, and international focus on the piracy problem in all of its forms could well be a major factor in reducing piracy in both quantity and quality. But that alone will not be enough.

Money and multinational assistance must continue to be provided to nations where maritime crime is a constant menace. If the problem is going to be solved, money and commitment are necessary over the long term.

And more than even the highly disputed use of lethal force against pirate attacks, at least on the high seas, may well be necessary to bring piracy under effective control.

Good intelligence should be able to both identify seagoing pirate groups and the places from which they operate. If there is sufficient international interest in getting at these people, then they can be appropriately targeted and attacked by naval, land, and air forces. Even these actions, given the mobility of pirates and their ability to hide, coupled with the reality that the most punishing military attacks will not be maintained for long periods, will not end piracy. But, in an age of "message sending," the communication to these maritime criminals, whatever they are called, will be abundantly clear.

Piracy is, after all, a very old criminal calling and a most persistent one. Historically, as with all aberrant and aggressive behavior, it has never been reduced through any process of negotiation. In the end, only the application of significant armed force has been successful in the suppression of pirates and piracy. Even the mass pardons of piracy's Golden Age as were granted under Woodes Rogers were effective because of the existence of overwhelming military force. One might note, even further, that no widespread violent criminal activity has ever been reduced by talking about it.

It may be that only a major piracy event that attracts world attention will generate the kind of action that will create and keep the pressure on pirates, particularly those operating on the high seas. One can only imagine, for example, a repeat of the SS *Mayaguez* incident in 1975 when that American ship and its crew were seized by a Cambodian patrol boat and held until President Ford sent the U.S. Marines to get them out. Add some dead or wounded Americans into such an unfortunate scenario and the significant level of response can be readily imagined.

And then consider a spill such as occurred at Valdez, but let it be the result of pirates seizing a ship that subsequently hits a tanker or, possibly, of such a seized and unmanned vessel plowing through crowded shipping lanes. That, too, would generate international interest in pirates and, presumably, a strong response directed against the perpetrators.

It is sincerely hoped that international leaders and those within the maritime community will not require screaming headlines and top-of-the-evening news television broadcasts to effectively deal with the piracy problem. But the potential for that is uncomfortably, indeed, perilously, high.

Notes

CHAPTER ONE. THE EVOLUTION OF PIRACY

1. Ormerod, *Piracy in the Ancient World*, 13.
2. Ibid.
3. Villiers, *Men, Ships and the Sea*, 29.
4. Ormerod, *Piracy in the Ancient World*, 55.
5. Ibid., 13.
6. Villiers, *Men, Ships and the Sea*, 55.
7. Andrews, *Elizabethan Privateering*, 3.
8. Villiers, *Men, Ships and the Sea*, 124.
9. Sherry, *Raiders and Rebels*, 84.
10. Ibid., 201–3.
11. *The Visual Dictionary of Ships and Sailing*, 12–13, 54.
12. Ibid., 14–15.
13. Sherry, *Raiders and Rebels*, 96–98.
14. *Collier's Encyclopedia*, 72–73.
15. Sherry, *Raiders and Rebels*, 117.
16. Kavenagh, *Foundations of Colonial America*, 321.
17. Sherry, *Raiders and Rebels*, 238.
18. Ibid., 76–78.
19. Ibid., 214–15.

20. Ibid., 182–83.
21. Ibid., 250–52.
22. Ibid., 34.
23. Villiers, *Men, Ships and the Sea,* 126.
24. Sherry, *Raiders and Rebels,* 360–62.
25. Rowe, "Report of Intruders Boarding Vessel at Anchor Off Santos, Brasil on 18 December 1988" (on file with the *Tulane Maritime Law Journal*).
26. "The Bloody Cost of Inaction," *Fairplay,* 3 September 1998, 24.
27. Adventura, "My Odyssey on M/S Marta," *Parola,* Philippine Seamen's Assistance Program, May/June 1993, 6,7.
28. Perot, "Daylight Robbery," *Via Inmarsat,* July 1997, 20.
29. Perot, "Daylight Robbery," 23.
30. "Pirates Kill Three Seafarers," *The Sea,* March/April 1993, 8.
31. Perot, "Daylight Robbery," 23.
32. "The Bloody Cost," 22–23.

CHAPTER TWO. PIRATES AND THE LAW

1. Lucie-Smith, *Outcasts of the Sea,* 8.
2. Paulsen, "An Historical Overview of the Development of Uniformity in International Maritime Law," 1065.
3. Geneva Convention on the High Seas (1958), Article 15.
4. Brittin, *International Law for Seagoing Officers,* 78–79.
5. Ibid., 123.
6. Geneva Convention on the Territorial Sea and Contiguous Zone (1958).
7. *United States Code,* Title 18, 1651–53.
8. Brittin, *International Law for Seagoing Officers,* 155.
9. Ibid., 155–56.
10. Stevenson and Oxman, Various reports on the Third United Nations Conference on the Law of the Sea, *American Journal of International Law,* 68, no. 1 (1974); 69, no. 4 (1975); 71, no. 2 (1977); 72, no. 1 (1978); 73, no. 1 (1979); 74, no. 1 (1980); 75, no. 2 (1981); 76, no. 1 (1982).
11. United Nations Conference on the Law of the Sea (1982), Article 101.

12. McGinley, "The *Achille Lauro* Affair—Implications for International Law," *Tennessee Law Review,* 1985, 691.

13. Klinghoffer v. S.N.C. *Achille Lauro* et al.

14. Halberstam, "Terrorism on the High Seas," 269, 289.

15. Constantinople, "Piracy and the Achille Lauro," 723, 750.

16. Gorman, "What Every Maritime Attorney Should Know About Modern-Day Piracy."

17. Chief Bosun Mate, USCGC BIBB 1979.

18. Klinghoffer v. S.N.C. *Achille Lauro* et al.

19. Clifford and Turchi, *The Pirate Price,* 21–73.

20. Ibid., 63–73.

21. DeConde, *A History of American Foreign Policy,* 83–85.

CHAPTER THREE. PIRATES AT WORK:
EUROPE AND THE AMERICAS

1. "Why a Big Surge in 'Boatnapping,' " 41.

2. "Drugs, Death Ride the Waves," 17.

3. Kryzanowicz, "Boaters Beware: Drug Hijack 'Season' Opens," 1.

4. Clancy, *Clear and Present Danger,* 17–18, 28–43.

5. Kryzanowicz, "Boaters Beware: Drug Hijack 'Season' Opens."

6. Benchley, *The Island,* 103.

7. Murphy, House Merchant Marine and Fisheries Committee, *Report on the Hijacking of U.S. Pleasure Yachts and Cabin Cruisers.*

8. Kryzanowicz, "Boaters Beware: Drug Hijack 'Season' Opens."

9. "Couple Survive Shootout at Sea with Pirates," 1.

10. "Caught in the Act," *Yachting,* 58–61.

11. U.S. Department of Transportation, *Maritime Security Report,* October 1997, 3.

12. Robles, "Police: Two Found Dead in River May Be Pirates," 1.

13. *Piracy and Armed Robbery against Ships,* International Maritime Bureau Annual Report (1996).

14. Ibid.

15. Grissim, "Yo-Ho-Ho, a Ski Mask and Gun," 1.

16. *Piracy and Armed Robbery against Ships* (1997).

17. *Piracy and Armed Robbery against Ships* (1996).

18. Ibid.

19. Ibid.
20. Ibid.
21. Moulier, "Pirates? What Pirates?" 33–34.
22. *Piracy and Armed Robbery against Ships* (1996).
23. Stevenson, 16 January 1996.
24. *Piracy and Armed Robbery against Ships* (1997).
25. Ibid.
26. Ibid.
27. Ibid.
28. U.S. Department of Transportation, *Maritime Security Report,* January 1996, 2.
29. *Piracy and Armed Robbery against Ships* (1997).
30. Ibid.
31. Ibid.
32. U.S. Department of Transportation, *Maritime Security Report,* October 1997, 2.
33. U.S. Department of Transportation, *Maritime Security Report,* January 1996, 2–3.
34. *Piracy and Armed Robbery against Ships* (1997).
35. Ibid.
36. Chaliand and Rageau, *Strategic Atlas,* 177.
37. U.S. Department of Transportation, *Maritime Security Report,* October 1997, 2.
38. Ibid.
39. Ibid., 4.
40. U.S. Department of Transportation, *Maritime Security Report,* January 1996, 8.
41. Ibid.
42. Ibid.

CHAPTER FOUR. PIRATES AT WORK: AFRICA AND SOUTHEAST ASIA

1. U.S. Department of Energy, *Piracy: The Threat to Tanker Traffic* (September 1992), 5.
2. Ibid., 7.
3. Gottschalk. *The Global Trade and Investment Handbook,* 491.
4. *Piracy and Armed Robbery against Ships* (1997).

5. Ibid.

6. Gottschalk, *The Global Trade and Investment Handbook,* 233.

7. *Piracy and Armed Robbery against Ships.*

8. Ibid.

9. Gottschalk, *The Global Trade and Investment Handbook,* 500.

10. *Piracy and Armed Robbery against Ships* (1997).

11. Ibid.

12. Ibid.

13. Ibid.

14. Ibid.

15. Ibid.

16. Ibid.

17. Ibid.

18. Ibid.

19. Ibid.

20. Gottschalk, *The Global Trade and Investment Handbook,* 341.

21. *Piracy and Armed Robbery against Ships* (1997). Information in the sections "Somalia" through "South China Sea" is drawn from this source.

22. Moulier, "Pirates? What Pirates?" 33–34.

23. Grissim, "Piracy Returns," 6.

24. Moulier, "Pirates? What Pirates?" 33–34.

25. Grissim, "Piracy Returns," 7.

26. Ibid.

27. Ibid.

28. Ibid.

CHAPTER FIVE. THE ECONOMIC COST

1. Ellen, fax to author, 17 August 1998.

2. Pieris, "Sea Wolves Feasting."

3. Farnham, "Pirates!"

4. *World Almanac and Book of Facts* (1997).

5. Williams, "Merchant Vessel Chartering and Operation in International Trade," 71–96.

6. Abhyankar, fax to author, 17 August 1998.

7. Wright, "Grappling with Modern Day Buccaneers: Lebanon Tries to Sink 'Paintbrush' Pirates."

8. Ellen.

9. Abhyankar.

10. *Piracy and Armed Robbery against Ships* (July 1998).

11. *Piracy and Armed Robbery against Ships* (March 1998).

12. *Piracy and Armed Robbery against Ships* (July 1998).

13. *Piracy and Armed Robbery against Ships* (March 1998).

14. *Piracy and Armed Robbery against Ships* (July 1998).

15. *Piracy and Armed Robbery against Ships* (March 1998).

16. 8a *American Jurisprudence* 2d, Bailments, Section 80.

17. Ibid.

18. Abhyankar.

19. Farnham, "Pirates!"

20. Drogin, "Pirates Setting Sail for New Plunder."

21. Williams, "Merchant Vessel Chartering and Operation in International Trade."

22. *Piracy and Armed Robbery against Ships* (March 1998).

23. Ibid.

24. Ibid.

25. Ellen, "Bringing Piracy to Account."

26. Marshall, fax to author, 2 September 1998.

27. Abhyankar.

28. Marshall.

29. Ibid.

30. Sullivan, "There's a Price to Pay for That Craft of Your Dreams."

31. *Piracy and Armed Robbery against Ships* (March 1998).

32. Farnham, "Pirates!"

33. *Piracy and Armed Robbery against Ships* (March 1998).

CHAPTER SIX. PIRATES, TERRORISTS, AND ENVIRONMENTAL HORRORS

1. *Montreal Daily Star,* 6 December 1917, 1.

2. *New York Times,* 17 April 1947, 1.

3. Greenbaum, "Texas City Is a Ghost Town in Shadow of Raging Fires," 1.

4. Jones, *Deadline Disaster,* 174–77.

5. *Piracy and Armed Robbery against Ships* (1997).

6. Moulier, "Pirates? What Pirates?" 33–34.

7. *Piracy: The Threat to Tanker Traffic.*

8. *Piracy and Armed Robbery against Ships.*

9. *Piracy: The Threat to Tanker Traffic.*

10. *Piracy and Armed Robbery against Ships.* Material in the sections "Some Terrorist Examples" through "More Lethal, Less Passive Means" is drawn from this source.

11. Ibid., 2.

12. NBC News, 1 June 1999.

13. Reuters, 11 March 1993 (and reported in above referenced DOE report—1993).

14. *Piracy: The Threat to Tanker Traffic.*

15. *Piracy and Armed Robbery against Ships.*

16. Ibid.

17. Ibid.

18. Ibid.

CHAPTER SEVEN. SOLUTIONS

1. Gorman, "What Every Maritime Attorney Should Know about Modern-Day Piracy," 9–10.

2. *Piracy: The Threat to Tanker Traffic,* 1.

3. Moulier, "Pirates? What Pirates?" 33–34.

4. *Pirates and Armed Robbers, A Master's Guide,* 1–3.

5. *Piracy and Armed Robbery against Ships* (1997).

6. Ibid.

7. Ibid.

8. Ibid.

9. Ibid.

10. Ibid.

11. Grissim, "Piracy Returns," 19.

12. Stevenson, "Piracy and the Mariner."

13. Conversation with anonymous source, 28 March 1998.

14. Stevenson, "Piracy and the Mariner."

15. Cheek, "'Supremely Simple': The Case for Sea Piracy," 2–3.

16. Schlesinger, "Pirates—Some in Uniform—Prowl the S. China Sea," 1.

17. U.S. Department of Transportation, *Maritime Security Report,* January 1996, 1–3.

18. Moulier, "Pirates? What Pirates?" 34.

19. Gorman, "What Every Maritime Attorney Should Know about Modern-Day Piracy," 3.

20. Healy and Sharpe, *Cases and Materials on Admiralty,* 616.

Bibliography

Abhyankar, Jayant. Fax to Dennis LaRochelle, 17 August 1998.

Adams, Charles M. *The Colonial Period of American History,* Vol. 4, *England's Commercial and Colonial Policy.* New Haven, Conn.: Yale University Press, 1938.

Adams, James Truslow. *A History of American Life,* Vol. 2, *Provincial Policy, 1690–1763.* New York: Macmillan and Company, 1928.

Adventura, Nette. "My Odyssey on M/S *Marta.*" *Parola* (Philippine Seamen's Assistance Program). Rotterdam: May/June 1993.

American Jurisprudence 2d. Vol. 8a. (Bailments, Section 80). Mahwah, N.J.: West Publishing Company, 1998.

Andrews, Kenneth R. *Elizabethan Privateering, English Privateering during the Spanish War, 1585–1603.* London: Cambridge University Press, 1964.

Benchley, Peter. *The Island.* Garden City, N.Y.: Doubleday & Company, Inc., 1979.

"Blasts and Fires Wreck Texas City of 15,000; 1,200 Feared Dead; Thousands Hurt, Homeless; Wide Coast Area Rocked, Damage in Millions." *New York Times,* 17 April 1947.

"The Bloody Cost of Inaction." *Fairplay,* Coulsdon, Surrey, UK, 3 September 1998.

Brittin, Burdick M. *International Law for Seagoing Officers.* 3d ed. Annapolis, Md.: Naval Institute Press, 1972.

"Caught in the Act." *Yachting,* March 1998, 58–61.

Chaliand, Gerard, and Jean-Pierre Rageau. *Strategic Atlas, A Comparative Geopolitics of the World's Powers.* 3d ed. New York: Harper Collins Publishers, 1992.

Cheek, Philip. "'Supremely Simple': The Case for Sea Piracy." Unpublished manuscript. Cited by Larry Kahn, "Pirates, Rovers, and Thieves: New Problem with an Old Enemy," *Tulane Maritime Law Journal* 30 (April 1995).

Clancy, Tom. *Clear and Present Danger.* New York: G.P. Putnam's Sons, 1989.

Clifford, Berry, and Peter Turchi. *The Pirate Prince.* New York: Simon & Schuster, 1993.

Constantinople, George R. "Towards a New Definition of Piracy: The Achille Lauro Incident." *Virginia Journal of International Law* 26 (1986).

"Couple Survive Shootout at Sea with Pirates." *News and Tribune,* Fort Pierce, Fl., 4 September 1992, 1.

DeConde, Alexander. *A History of American Foreign Policy.* 2d ed. New York: Charles Scribner's Sons, 1971.

Drogin, Bob. "Pirates Setting Sail for New Plunder." *Los Angeles Times,* 27 November 1990.

"Drugs, Death Ride the Waves." *National Observer,* 8 February 1975, 17.

Ellen, Eric. "Bringing Piracy to Account." *Jane's Navy International,* 1 April 1997.

―――. Fax to Dennis LaRochelle, 17 August 1998.

Farnham, Alan. "Pirates!" *Fortune,* 15 July 1991.

Geneva Convention on the High Seas (1958), Article 15.

Geneva Convention on the Territorial Sea and Contiguous Zone (1958).

Gorman, Frances J. "What Every Maritime Attorney Should Know about Modern-Day Piracy." Baltimore, Md., 10 September 1993.

Goss, Philip. "Piracy and Buccaneering." *Collier's Encyclopedia.* New York: Collier's, 1993.

Gottschalk, Jack A. *The Global Trade and Investment Handbook.* Chicago: Probus Publishing Co., 1993.

Greenbaum, Lucy. "Texas City Is a Ghost Town in Shadow of Raging Fires." *New York Times,* 18 April 1947.

Grissim, John. "Piracy Returns." *Coast Guard,* September 1997, 6.

———. "Yo-Ho-Ho, a Ski Mask and Gun." *Washington Post,* 22 June 1997, 1.

Halberstam, David. "Terrorism on the High Seas: The *Achille Lauro*—Piracy and the IMO Convention on Marine Safety." *American Journal of International Law* 82 (1998).

"Halifax Wrecked by Explosion." *Montreal Daily Star,* 6 December 1917.

Hawke, David. *The Colonial Experience.* New York: The Bobbs-Merrill Co., Inc., 1966.

Healy, Nicholas J., and David J. Sharpe. *Cases and Materials on Admiralty.* St. Paul, Minn.: West Publishing Co., 1974.

Jones, Michael Wynn. *Deadline Disaster.* Chicago, Ill.: Henry Regnery Co., 1976.

Kavenagh, W. Keith. *Foundations of Colonial America: A Documentary History.* New York: Chelsea House, 1973.

Kryzanowicz, Marianne. "Boaters Beware: Drug Hijack 'Season' Opens." *Evening Capital,* 1 October 1980.

The Lore of Ships. New York: W.H. Smith Publishers, Inc., 1990.

Lucie-Smith, Edward. *Outcasts of the Sea.* New York: Paddington Press, 1978.

Marshall, Matthew. Fax to Dennis LaRochelle, 2 September 1998.

McGinley, Gerald P. "The *Achille Lauro* Affair—Implications for International Law." *Tennessee Law Review* 53 (1985).

Morison, Samuel Elliot. *The Maritime History of Massachusetts.* Boston: Houghton Mifflin Company, 1921.

Moulier, Phillipe. "Pirates? What Pirates? *U.S. News and World Report,* 23 June 1997, 33–34.

Ormerod, Henry A. *Piracy in the Ancient World: An Essay in Mediterranean History.* Baltimore, Md.: Johns Hopkins University Press, 1997.

Paulsen, Gordon W. "An Historical Overview of the Development of Uniformity in International Maritime Law." *Tulane Law Review* 57(1983).

Perot, Vivienne. "Daylight Robbery." *Via Inmarsat,* July 1997, 20–23.

Pieris, Harold. "Sea Wolves Feasting." *The WorldPaper Online,* May 1997.

Piracy and Armed Robbery against Ships. International Maritime Bureau Annual Report. Barking, UK (1996, 1997, 1998).

Pirates and Armed Robbers, A Master's Guide. London: International Shipping Federation, 1996.

"Pirates Kill Three Seafarers." *The Sea,* March/April 1993, 8

Robles, Frances. "Police: Two Found Dead in River May Be Pirates." *Miami Herald,* 27 January 1998.

Rowe, J. F. "Report of Intruders Boarding Vessel at Anchor off Santos, Brasil on 18 December 1988." (On file with the *Tulane Marine Law Journal.*)

Schlesinger, David. "Pirates—Some in Uniform—Prowl the S. China Sea." *Journal of Commerce,* 10 July 1995.

Sherry, Frank. *Raiders and Rebels: The Golden Age of Piracy.* New York: Hearst Marine Books, 1986.

Stevenson, Douglas B. Internal memo, 16 January 1996.

———. "Piracy and the Mariner." Address to the Mariner's Museum Conference, Newport News, Va., 15 November 1997.

Sullivan, Aline. "There's a Price to Pay for That Craft of Your Dreams." *International Herald Tribune,* 24 May 1997.

U.S. Bureau of the Census. *Statistical Abstract.* Washington, D.C., 1991, 1992, 1994, 1996.

U.S. Department of Commerce. *Ecological Study of the Amoco Cadiz Oil Spill.* Report of the NOAA-CNEXO Joint Scientific Commission. Washington, D.C., 1982.

U.S. Department of Energy. *Piracy: The Threat to Tanker Traffic.* Washington, D.C., September 1992; March 1993.

U.S. Department of Transportation. Office of Ports and Domestic Shipping. *Maritime Security Report.* Washington, D.C., January 1996; October 1997.

U.S. House of Representatives. Merchant Marine and Fisheries Committee. *Report on the Hijacking of U.S. Pleasure Yachts and Cabin Cruisers.* Washington, D.C., 27 August 1974.

United Nations Conference on the Law of the Sea, Article 101 (1982).

United States Code, Title 18.

Villiers, Alan. *Men, Ships and the Sea.* Washington, D.C.: National Geographic Survey, 1973.

The Visual Dictionary of Ships and Sailing. New York: Dorling Kindersley, Inc., 1991.

"Why a Big Surge in 'Boatnapping.'" *U.S. News & World Report,* 27 February 1978, 41.

Williams, E. Cameron. "Merchant Vessel Chartering and Operation in International Trade: Ethical and Safety Issues." *International Journal of Commerce and Management* 6(1996), 71–96.

World Almanac and Book of Facts. Mahwah, N.J.: World Almanac Books, 1995, 1997, 1998.

Wright, Robin. "Grappling with Modern-Day Buccaneers: Lebanon Tries to Sink 'Paintbrush' Pirates." *Christian Science Monitor* (Midwestern ed.), 13 July 1992.

Index

Egypt, *Achille Lauro* and, 37
Ellen, Eric, 86, 88–89, 99, 104
environmental catastrophe, maritime, 105–6, 107; explosions, 109–11; international intelligence program and, 124; running aground incidents, 111–13
Esperanza, 66
Essex, USS, 43
Europe, piracy in, 54–55
Every, Henry, 12–13
excess insurance, 102
Exxon Valdez oil spill, 105, 112, 146

Fair Lady, 55
Fancy, 12
Far East, piracy in, 78
Fateh Mohamed, 13
Feeling, 55
fences. *See* merchant fences
Finnsnes, 69
fire hoses, 119, 122
fiscal laws, 33
Fischland, 67
Fisher, 41
fishermen, modern piracy and, 52
flags, pirate, 8–9
Florida, pirates in, 53–54
Ford, Gerald, 146
Fortune, 77
Fortune (magazine), 105

Galvano, Captain, 34
Gambia, piracy in, 64
Gang-I-Sawai, 13
Gebruder Winter, 25
Geneva Conventions on Fisheries (1958), 32
Geneva Conventions on the Continental Shelf (1958), 32

Geneva Conventions on the High Seas (1958), 32; piracy exceptions to, 32–33; Third United Nations Conference on the Law of the Sea and, 36
Geneva Conventions on the Territorial Sea and Contiguous Zone (1958), 32
Ghana, piracy in, 67
Glory II, 83
Golden Age of piracy, 4, 7–20; Caribbean and, 44; crew discipline of, 9–10; merchant fences of, 11; pardons of, 19–20, 145; perils of, 11–12; pirates of, 12–19; ship flags of, 8–9; ships of, 7–8; targets of, 10–11
Gold Spring, 73
Got-Cha-Covered, 78
government(s): corruption in, 61, 62, 139–40; counterterrorism and, 131; piracy costs and, 104–6; piracy intervention by, 106–8; piracy reports and, 122
Grandcamp explosion, 111
Great Calm, 121
Greece: Coast Guard of, 55; piracy in, 54
Guyana, piracy in, 56

Hague Convention on Suppression of Unlawful Seizure of Aircraft, 38
Haiti, port security in, 128–29
Halifax, Nova Scotia, ship collision, 110, 123
Hanseatic League, 2, 31
hazard pay, 96
Hedges, Charles, 31
Helena, 70, 130

Hijacking of U.S. Pleasure Yachts and Cabin Cruisers Report to House Merchant Marine and Fisheries Committee (1970s), 49
hijackings: airplane, 35; pirate attack, 88; unreported pirate attack, 89. *See also* yachtjacking
Hispaniola, privateers on, 4
Hye Mieko, 116

Ibn Qutaibah, 76
Ilya Ehrenburg, 58, 59–60
Imo collides with *Mont Blanc,* 110
indemnification protection, 98
India, piracy in, 71
Indian Ocean, piracy in, 70–71
Indonesia: antipiracy efforts in, 144; hull insurance in, 104; piracy in, 73–75
insurance/insurers, 94–95; early methods for, 101–2; fraud, boat disappearances and, 50–51; piracy costs for, 100–104; piracy deterrence and, 141–43; piracy risk for, 103; policy deductibles of, 89, 95–96, 102–3; premiums for, 103–4; types of, 102
intelligence: international, 124, 131, 145; in ports, 129
International Chamber of Commerce, 23, 86, 140
International Court of Justice, 30
International Federation of Ship Owners, 141
international law, public, 30
International Maritime Bureau (IMB), 24, 143–44; *Anna Sierra* scam and, 82; on armed defense, 134; Brazilian piracy and, 59, 60; environmental

catastrophe concern of, 105–6; on European piracy in 1997, 54–55; expanded piracy definition of, 109, 114–15, 126–27; media support for, 53; on *Petro Ranger* hijacking, 26; on Philippines piracy, 77; *Piracy and Armed Robbery Against Ships,* 57, 93; on piracy attacks, 1995, 87; reports of pirate attacks and, 122; on Sri Lankan piracy, 73; on terrorists, 123. *See also* Regional Piracy Centre, IMB
International Maritime Organization, UN, 89; Maritime Safety Committee of, 118, 140
International Police Organization (Interpol), 60
International Shipping Federation, 97, 134
International Transport Worker's Federation, 141
Iran, piracy in, 71
The Island (Benchley), 48–49
Italy, 38–39; *Achille Lauro* and, 37; Coast Guard of, 55; organized crime in, 60; piracy in, 54
Ivan Chernych, 54–55
Ivory Coast, piracy in, 67

Jahan, 67, 83
Japanese pirates, 2–3
Julius Caesar, 1–2
jurisdictions, territorial, 32–33, 34

Kamillii, 45
Kamillo Sjenfuegoss, 56
Kapitan Betkher, 56
Kidd, William, 3, 12, 15–17

murder at sea, 24–25; law on, 30
Murphy, John, 49
Myannmar, piracy in, 76–77

Nadia J, 67–68, 113–14
Nagasaki Spirit collision with
    Ocean Blessing, 113
Nandu Arrow, 117
Napetco I, 66
National Commission for Public
    Security in the Ports,
    Terminals, and Waterways
    (Brazil, 1995), 59
navigation, improvements in,
    6–7
Navigation Acts, 18
Navy, U.S.: *Achille Lauro* and,
    37; Barbary pirates and,
    42–43; *Santa Maria* piracy
    investigation by, 34–35
'Ndragheta (organized crime), 60
Nedlloyd Steenkirk, 64
Nelvana, 25
New Providence island,
    Bahamas, 5
Nigeria: piracy in, 64, 67–68;
    port security in, 128
Nordfarer, 58
Normar Splendour, 73
North African pirates, 3
Northerly-Island, 65
northern waters, piracy in, 53
North Sea, 73
Nuova Lloydiana, 72

Ocean Blessing collision with
    Nagasaki Spirit, 113
Office of Trade and Economic
    Analysis, U.S., 87
Oleron, Rules of, 31
organized crime, 60, 61–62
Oriental Bright, 75

Oscar Venture, 79
Ottoman Turks, 3

Paccini III, 78
Palestine Liberation
    Organization (PLO), 36–37,
    39–40, 115
Panama, 131
Papua New Guinea, piracy in, 78
Paramushir, 78
Permanent International Court
    of Justice at the Hague, 30
Persian Gulf, pirates in, 3
Peru, piracy in, 56, 57
Petrobulk Racer, 74–75
Petro Ranger, 26, 80
phantom ships, 63–64, 67, 81–84
Philadelphia, USS, 43
Philip Channel, Southeast Asia,
    105–6, 114, 144
Philippines: antipiracy efforts in,
    121, 144; piracy in, 77–78;
    port security in, 128
Pieris, Harold, 86
Pioneer, 79–80
piracy, modern: culture of,
    52–53; on high seas, 129–31;
    law regarding, 28–43; scope
    of, 20–24; violence of, 24, 57,
    83–84, 96; yachtjacking and,
    44–45, 47–50. *See also*
    antipiracy measures; armed
    self-defense; defense mea-
    sures; economic costs of
    piracy
*Piracy and Armed Robbery Against
    Ships,* 57, 93
pirate(s): motivation for, 6–7,
    125–26; requirements for suc-
    cess as, 5–6; *versus* terrorists,
    122–24, 131. *See also* defini-
    tions, piracy

pirate attacks: reporting, 121–22, 141; types of, 87–88, 89 (table); unreported, 88–89; weapons used in, 121. *See also* antipiracy measures

Pirate Museum, Provincetown, Mass., 42

police, uniformed, 129

Poloflat, 70

Pompey the Great, 2

Porer, 117

port(s), 118–19, 128–29, 131

Port Chicago, Cal. explosion, 110

Preble, Edward, 43

President, USS, 43

privateers, 3–5, 7, 125, 136

Product Queen, 80

Proteus, 66

punishment for piracy, 120–21

Queen Anne's Revenge, 12

Rackam, John "Calico Jack," 12, 14

Rahah, 80

Rajah Brooke, 72

Rakam, 77

Ratana Sopa, 78

Read, Mary, 12, 14

Reagan, Ronald, 37

rebels, 63–64

Red Cross, International Committee of, 72

Red Sea, piracy in, 70

Regional Piracy Centre, IMB, 87, 97, 98, 140–41

Rejane Delmas, 69

Renalo, 54

resistance to piracy: economic cost of, 86–94

Rhodes (Greek island): early

maritime law of, 1; early merchants, "general averaging" for losses of, 101

Rio Amazonia, 57

Rita, 121

robbery, 61–62; as piracy, 53–54; at sea, law on, 30

Rogers, Woodes, 19, 145

ROTC cadets' (radar) blip incident, 46–47

Rugen, 67

Sacra Corona Unita (organized crime), 60

Safe Navigation Committee of the Asian Shipowners' Forum, 97

Sagittarius, 55

sanitary laws, 33

San Marino, 56, 117–18

Santa Maria, 34–35

satellite-based piracy tracking, 139

scams, maritime, 63–64, 81–84

Scarborough, HMS, 12

Schute, Samuel, 41

Scoff, 69

Seagull, 55

Seaman's Church Institute, 134, 141

Seaway, 66

Senegal, piracy in, 64, 65

Shandeline, 53, 119

ship operators, piracy reports by, 141

shipping industry, 94–98; antipiracy efforts of, 97–98; bailment laws and, 94; cargo protection and, 116–18; delay/loss risks for, 96–97; hazard pay and, 96; marine insurance and, 94–95

ships, pirate, 7, 8

About the Authors

Jack A. Gottschalk is an attorney and consultant with three decades of experience in journalism, television, and public relations. He has lectured at the Medill School of Journalism, Northwestern University, written on subjects ranging from international trade to mass communications, and produced and hosted *Legally Speaking*, a Comcast television presentation from 1993 to 1996. Mr. Gottschalk earned an undergraduate degree in journalism. He holds a law degree and graduate degrees in general management and international relations. This is his seventh book.

Brian P. Flanagan is a graduate of Tufts University and received his law degree from Catholic University of America. He was commissioned in the U.S. Coast Guard and served on active duty with assignments to the U.S. Department of State and in the Operational Law Enforcement Division at Coast Guard Headquarters, as well as aboard ship. He has been an adjunct professor of admiralty law at Suffolk University Law School since 1989 and is a proctor member of the Maritime Law Association of the United States. He practices admiralty law in Boston.

Lawrence J. Kahn has written and lectured widely on the subject of admiralty law and maritime crime. He is a graduate of Columbia University and received his law degree from Tulane University. From 1995 to 1998, Mr. Kahn was the staff attorney for the Center for Seafarer's Rights in New York City. He now practices law in New York City.

Dennis M. LaRochelle is a 1982 graduate of the U.S. Naval Academy and served aboard the USS *George Washington Carver* (SSBN 656 Gold) through 1987. He graduated *cum laude* from Harvard Law School in 1996 and currently practices law in New York City.

The Naval Institute Press is the book-publishing arm of the U.S. Naval Institute, a private, nonprofit, membership society for sea service professionals and others who share an interest in naval and maritime affairs. Established in 1873 at the U.S. Naval Academy in Annapolis, Maryland, where its offices remain today, the Naval Institute has members worldwide.

Members of the Naval Institute support the education programs of the society and receive the influential monthly magazine *Proceedings* and discounts on fine nautical prints and on ship and aircraft photos. They also have access to the transcripts of the Institute's Oral History Program and get discounted admission to any of the Institute-sponsored seminars offered around the country.

The Naval Institute also publishes *Naval History* magazine. This colorful bimonthly is filled with entertaining and thought-provoking articles, first-person reminiscences, and dramatic art and photography. Members receive a discount on *Naval History* subscriptions.

The Naval Institute's book-publishing program, begun in 1898 with basic guides to naval practices, has broadened its scope in recent years to include books of more general interest. Now the Naval Institute Press publishes about one hundred titles each year, ranging from how-to books on boating and navigation to battle histories, biographies, ship and aircraft guides, and novels. Institute members receive discounts of 20 to 50 percent on the Press's more than eight hundred books in print.

Full-time students are eligible for special half-price membership rates. Life memberships are also available.

For a free catalog describing Naval Institute Press books currently available, and for further information about subscribing to *Naval History* magazine or about joining the U.S. Naval Institute, please write to:

Membership Department
U.S. Naval Institute
291 Wood Road
Annapolis, MD 21402-5034
Telephone: (800) 233-8764
Fax: (410) 269-7940
Web address: www.usni.org